Sociology and Management Education

While examining the intersections and engagements between sociology and management education in historical and contemporary terms, this slim volume outlines the agenda of a promising prospective engagement between the two. It specifically foregrounds the Indian experience without being indifferent to the global context that has shaped the unprecedented rise of business schools. Employing a perspective from the Global South, it contextualises the dominance of the US model of management curriculum and disciplinary practices in relation to wider geopolitics of knowledge production. Parenthetically, it presents a critical assessment of Indian scholarly contributions to the field of management studies. This book should be of interest to management educators, administrators, and sociologists besides the students and researchers in the broad area of organisation studies.

Manish Thakur is Professor at the Public Policy and Management Group, Indian Institute of Management Calcutta, Kolkata.

Routledge Focus on Management and Society
Series Editor: **Anindya Sen**, Professor of Economics, Indian Institute of Management Calcutta, Kolkata, West Bengal, India

The invisible hand of market has today been replaced by the visible hand of managerial capitalism. As the power and role of the managers have expanded, the world also has become more dynamic and volatile. To run their organisations more efficiently, the managers need to be aware of new developments taking place all around them. The Focus series addresses this need by presenting a number of short volumes that deal with important managerial issues in the Indian context. Volumes in the series will cover topics not only of perennial interest to managers but also emerging areas of interest like neuromarketing. Some of the well-established areas of research like bottom-of-the-pyramid marketing will be dealt with specifically in the Indian context, as well as critical developments in other fields, like Auction Theory.

The series is designed to introduce management theorists and researchers (as well as the lay public) to a diverse set of topics relevant directly or peripherally to management in a concise format without sacrificing basic rigour.

Other Books in this series

Excellence in Supply Chain Management
Balram Avittathur and Debabrata Ghosh

Digital Cultures
Smeeta Mishra

For a full list of titles in this series, please visit: https://www.routledge.com/Routledge-Focus-on-Management-and-Society/book-series/RFMS

Sociology and Management Education
Engagements and Agendas

Manish Thakur

First published 2022
by Routledge
2 Park Square, Milton Park, Abingdon, Oxon OX14 4RN

and by Routledge
605 Third Avenue, New York, NY 10158

Routledge is an imprint of the Taylor & Francis Group, an informa business

© 2022 Manish Thakur

The right of Manish Thakur to be identified as author of this work has been asserted in accordance with sections 77 and 78 of the Copyright, Designs and Patents Act 1988.

All rights reserved. No part of this book may be reprinted or reproduced or utilised in any form or by any electronic, mechanical, or other means, now known or hereafter invented, including photocopying and recording, or in any information storage or retrieval system, without permission in writing from the publishers.

Trademark notice: Product or corporate names may be trademarks or registered trademarks, and are used only for identification and explanation without intent to infringe.

British Library Cataloguing-in-Publication Data
A catalogue record for this book is available from the British Library

Library of Congress Cataloging-in-Publication Data
A catalog record has been requested for this book

ISBN: 9781032191089 (hbk)
ISBN: 9781032191171 (pbk)
ISBN: 9781003257813 (ebk)

DOI: 10.4324/9781003257813

Typeset in Times
by KnowledgeWorks Global Ltd.

For Amrendra *Mama*, in gratitude

&

Chutkun, in friendship

Contents

Preface		viii
Acknowledgements		xi
1	Introduction: Sociology and management education	1
2	Becoming a science: The quest for academic respectability	14
3	Meandering pathways: Betwixt the national and the global	41
4	Privileging critique: Sociology and its metamorphosis into critical management studies	68
5	Conclusion: Disciplinarity, inter-disciplinarity, and the new academy	94
References		102
Index		112

Preface

At a personal level, this book is an attempt to make sense of my institutional shift from a department of sociology of an Indian University (Goa) to an Indian Institute of Management (Calcutta). However, it is not about an aspect of my intellectual biography alone. Nor is it a free-flowing narrative of purely personal experiences of mine as a sociologist. At a time when the academic world is increasingly subjected to the spirited demands of *reflexivity*, I go back to C. Wright Mills' classic *The Sociological Imagination* (1959) as any old-fashioned student of sociology would do to remind myself of the need to cultivate 'the awareness of the relationship between personal experience and the wider society' (1959: 5). In fact, students of sociology are enjoined to self-consciously develop an outlook on life that involves a deep understanding of the intersectionality of one's biography and the historically embedded social processes. It is this appreciation of the necessary interplay of the individual and the larger social context that constitutes what Mills evocatively termed *the sociological imagination*. It means a cultivated ability of a person to 'think ourselves away from our daily routines and look at them anew' while connecting 'personal troubles to public issues' (1959: 7). Viewed thus, this book is an attempt to sociologically look at the historically evolving relationship between sociology and management as academic disciplines dotting the contemporary institutional landscape of higher education.

Indeed, an implicit engagement with elements of my intellectual biography animates this endeavour to illuminate the intricacies of relationships between the changing fortunes of two related disciplines – sociology and management. For years now, I have spent a great deal of time thinking, reading, and occasionally writing about the ways in which the two disciplines of sociology and management could speak to and benefit from each other. In 2010, I published an interim reflection on the relationship between sociology and management in the specific context of the Indian Institutes of Management (IIMs), which appeared in a collection of essays edited by Maitrayee Chaudhuri under the title *Sociology in India: Intellectual and Institutional Practices*. In hindsight, that essay appears a rambling lament of a young sociologist on the lookout for disciplinary certitude. A few years later, in 2017, as a co-editor (with my colleague R. Rajesh Babu) of the volume titled *Management Education in India: Perspectives and Practices*, I gained significant insights into the general relationship between management and related academic disciplines. I also got a wider perspective on the history of management education in India. Yet, as the title itself reveals, my thinking remained largely India-centric. The current volume amplifies some of these earlier themes in new ways. Unavoidably, there are certain repetition of ideas and themes across chapters. However, the book is refreshingly novel in its conceptualisation and execution and not a compendium of old (albeit revisited) ideas.

Firstly, this book dwells on the larger framework of disciplinary history to delineate the intersections and engagements between sociology and management education in the global context. As part of this framework, it outlines the historical quest of academic-scientific respectability on the part of both sociology and management studies and their implications for the mutual relationship. It particularly focuses on the US experience, for the latter has/had disproportionate influence on the standardisation and benchmarking of management curriculum and its disciplinary practices in general. The dominance of the US experience is also a perpetual reminder of the inherent asymmetries in the geopolitics of global knowledge production. Secondly, the book underlines the need to foreground epistemologies of the Global South as a serious antidote to Western ethnocentrism. There is no escaping from the serious interrogation of the American/Western empirical material, cases, models and theoretical apparatuses, and their uncritical application to non-Western settings. The plea here is not to close off one's door and windows on the outside world but to be alive to the power dynamics of the extant terms of intellectual engagement between the dominant and the dominated. Encouragingly, a movement emanating from the 'business schools' known by the name of Critical Management Studies (CMS) has provided us with a forum to question the taken-for-grantedness of the dominant global and explore alternative avenues of ideological and organisational resistance.

Lastly, the present volume is not intended as an undergraduate/postgraduate course book or textbook. Neither is it about histories of sociology and/or management studies. It is a well-considered reflection on contemporary disciplinary practices and the way they shape up the intellectual-institutional interface between two academic disciplines – one relatively older (sociology) and the other comparatively younger (management studies). In this sense, the book should be read as an invitation to a dialogue on various kinds of disciplinary entanglements that the institutional transformations of the global academy have orchestrated (or precluded).

Acknowledgements

Any piece of academic writing is seldom a solitary affair. The ideas animating a given work carry sediments of one's past works and the imprint of ongoing conversations with peers, friends, colleagues, and students. They also carry implicitly the elements of one's biography. I am acutely aware that this short reflection on the changing relationship between sociology and management would not have been possible without my shift to the Indian Institute of Management Calcutta (IIMC) in 2007. Previously, I taught for almost a decade at the University Department of Sociology at Goa. The move to IIMC has been productive for me in many ways. Indeed, IIMC has been known for its deep anchorage in social sciences making it more than an ordinary 'business school'. Self-consciously, IIMC has fashioned itself as an institution imparting management education with the latter encompassing the widest possible valence. Moreover, the well-imbibed institutional ethos of collegiality, and an egalitarian organisational culture of IIMC, has encouraged conversations across disciplines and age-cohorts.

This book owes its origins to one particular type of conversation – the post-lunch *adda* in the Faculty Lounge of the Institute where Prof. Anindya Sen, the Series Editor for the *Routledge Focus on Management and Society*, would be the key protagonist. Amidst meandering light-hearted banter on a range of issues (from the supposedly pretentious cultural configuration of *Bangaliana* (Bengaliness) to the capacious nature of early twentieth-century Bengali literature, from the decline of Kolkata as a city to the efflorescence of north Indian culinary traditions in West Bengal, from the increasingly narrower remit of microeconomics to the rise of post-modernism-infested heavy jargons in contemporary sociology, and the list goes on), sometime in 2017, Anindya da suggested to me the idea of writing this book. I immediately jumped on the offer without doing much for a long time. But then, being a seasoned

xii *Acknowledgements*

editor that he is, Anindya da has his own ways of gently nudging contributors. It was his patience, understanding and cordial reminders that made me work on this long-delayed project. I am immensely grateful to him for having kept his faith alive in the possibility of this work despite my sluggishness. This is also an occasion to acknowledge the goodwill and encouragement of our other *adda* mates at the Faculty Lounge from whom I have learnt so much: Amit Dhiman, Anirvan Pant, Bhaskar Chakrabarti, Biju Paul Abraham, Mritiunjoy Mohanty, Partha Ray, Rajiv Kumar, Rajesh Babu, Rajesh Bhattacharya, Runa Sarkar, Saikat Maitra, Soumen Sikdar, Sumanta Basu and Vidyanand Jha. Awaneesh was a source of camaraderie in the initial months of lockdown in Kolkata while I was working on this book.

Part of the writing for this book was done in Goa, the place with which I have had a long association, and where I had warm hospitality, cheerful company and full support from family, friends and well-wishers. I thank Aparajita Gangopadhyay, Maria Auroro Couto, Peter Ronald DeSouza, Koshy Tharakan, Rahul Tripathi, Prakash Desai, Ganesha Somayaji and Joanna Pereira for their generosity and sage advice.

This book being a product of shared ideas and insights, I have to acknowledge my debts to friends and colleagues spread across disciplines and cities: Arun Patnaik and Sasheej Hegde in Hyderabad; Muhammad Shakil, Mufsin P. P., Shoma Choudhury and Ujjayan Bhattacharya in Kolkata; Maitrayee Chaudhuri, Nabanipa Bhattacharjee, Shumona Goel, Dev Pathak and Bhaskarjit Neog in New Delhi; N. Jayaram, Manoj Kumar and Priyanshu Gupta in Bengaluru, Sujata Patel in Pune; Sadan Jha in Surat; Gyanendra Yadav in Patna; Mithilesh Dwivedy, Kalpana Pandey, Kumud Pandey, Kaushik Pandey and Kautuk Pandey in Madhubani; Irfan Ahmad and Rizwan Ahmad in Gottingen and Doha respectively; Paramjit Judge in Amritsar; Satish Sharma in Chandigarh; Satyan Jha in Paris. It was a pleasure working with Aafreen Ayub at Routledge whose professionalism facilitated this publication despite all round disruption caused by the pandemic.

I dedicate this book to Shri Amrendra Chaudhary, my *mama*, whose numerous acts of kindness opened up a new and exciting world for me by way of my admission to JNU, New Delhi, in 1990. I remain grateful to him and wish him a healthy and productive life. This book is also dedicated to Chutkun, whose friendship I cherish, and hope that as he grows, he will be able to appreciate the value of the printed word, something I learnt from Amrendra *mama*.

Kolkata Manish Thakur
21 July 2021

1 Introduction
Sociology and management education

Management education has come to acquire unprecedented public esteem and global currency in contemporary times. This was not always the case, though. As a programme of professional education, it had to face stiff resistance from various quarters in the early years of its origins. Critics of capitalism chastised it for its unequivocal identification with the profit-seeking motives of the corporate firms and their greedy shareholders. Defenders of the scholarly ethos of the modern academy looked down upon it for its vocationalism and academic shallowness. It was taken to be a part of the ideological project of modern capitalism meant to eulogise the virtues of corporate management. It was considered to be a ploy and a strategy to raise the (rather low) social status of businessmen and business managers in relation to other established professional groups. It was held to be acting as a prestigious platform to impart ethical legitimacy to the managers and their occupation. It was seen performing the functions of a finishing school to add the credential-based capital to the upwardly mobile aspirations of an occupational group wishing to be a respectable profession. Critics do talk about its identification and alignment with a particular set of interests as well, and in popular perception, even today, business schools are seen as embodying and furthering corporate interests. Many years ago, Baritz (1960) coined the evocative term *servants of power* to describe the way business schools functioned.

The wheels have turned a full circle now. Over time management education developed its own sophisticated repertoire of techniques, language, and values, and later, metamorphosed into a scholarly discipline with claims to scientific status with institutional approbation. In recent years, the idea of management (or, alternatively, the ideology of managerialism) has come to enjoy such prestige that its extension is sought to ever newer domains of collective and public life. That quintessential rational modern organisation of bureaucracy is being subjected

DOI: 10.4324/9781003257813-1

to the imperative of new public management and is increasingly under pressure to learn integrated notions of leadership, negotiation, conflict, and team building. The centrality of the idea of management to a wider vision of organisational and public life can be gauged from the substantial financial support institutions of management receive from corporations, philanthropists, and the public exchequer across the world. This support surely demonstrates the growing public belief in the perceived need for the greater deployment and wider expansion of management knowledge in society at large. For many, managerial competence is a neutral set of skills that can be used in pursuit of values of all kinds and in all sectors, both government and private. Some others look at modern management as a system of knowledge that reproduces the values and ethos of the market principle.

It is interesting to note that management education did bring in an air of democratic egalitarianism when it cast itself in opposition to the supposedly entrenched privileges of older elite professions: 'Management is the way in which "arrogant doctors" and public sector "elites" may be made accountable' (Grey 2002: 496). Ironically, management education, in due course, became the prime mechanism for creating and sustaining a new class of elites: the well-educated manager (Livingston 1971), the consultant, the investment banker, and the like. It evolved into an exclusive club of newly professionalised elites with a shared discursive and semiotic universe of its own. Sociologically speaking, the institutions of management, through their socialisation processes, contribute to the production of shared languages and understandings among managers. Such shared languages stem from wider cultural and political trends that legitimate the former and, in turn, get legitimated by them. In other words, a meaningful discussion of management education needs to factor in the ideological terrain of which it is part.

Owing to a favourable conjuncture of circumstances, management education has become the most favoured form of academic credential and public prestige as compared to other degrees and diplomas. Expectedly, there is an ascendance of the idea of management as a public good and management education as a valued professional training. No wonder that management education has witnessed a spectacular demand over the past half a century. Observers are quick to associate the spurt in demand for management education to the ultimate triumph of the hegemonic ideology of the market, particularly after the collapse of the erstwhile Union of Soviet Socialist Republics (USSR) and the associated doctrine of socialist industrialism. In any case, management education does offer status and credentials to individuals and helps them gain entry into lucrative organisational employment in our times. The institutions of management produce employable personnel for consultancies, investment banks, the public sector, and private industries. However, to brand them all as the unapologetic mouthpiece for a coherent set of business interests is to underplay the variegated nature of management education. Notwithstanding the abundance of literature on the purpose and value of management education, there is hardly a convincing collective narrative of management education in the 21st century. Of course, that does not deter hundreds of management institutions in India (and elsewhere) to act as mass production teaching factories as there is demand for their services in the market. There exists a variety of institutions of management with varying missions, goals, and objectives catering to diverse student bodies both nationally and internationally. They also differ in terms of the quality of education that they impart and the quality of the faculty that they employ. What binds them all though is their easy and largely uncritical acceptance of the United States as the fount of management knowledge and the ultimate reference model for academic and institutional emulation. The United States continues to exert enormous homogenising thrust on institutions of management globally amidst incessant discourses of a new compact between business, corporations, society, and business schools. The growing trends of international accreditation and rankings further strengthen the hold of the dominant U.S. model and weaken the quest for alternatives to the underlying philosophy of management education.

Be that as it may, institutions of management nowadays, are substantial academic-professional institutions in their own right with their ranking systems and accreditation bodies. Management studies produce their own Ph.Ds. and have come to replace its earlier status of an academically aspiring yet fledgling discipline with a confident branch of knowledge internally divided into sub-branches or sub-disciplines. In the process, it is ceding the earlier type of heterodoxy when a diverse range of interests and forms of understanding borrowed from well-established foundational disciplines in social and mathematical sciences were shaping its scholarly orientations and contents. With the institutional efflorescence of management education, now it is the turn of the well-established social science disciplines to make a case for their usefulness and relevance to management.

That is why it is not enough to simply join the bandwagon of management education as a trained sociologist, but to demonstrate as to how one's social scientific orientation and knowledge base fits in with the overall institutional matrix of management education and as to how a given sociological approach or a set of substantive topics may get related in matters of teaching and research in areas, such as organisational behaviour, human resources management, or business environment. In other words, the related disciplines of management have to continually prove their legitimacy in the context of management education. This is already happening as social scientists increasingly publish in management journals and write for management conferences (some write for only the Academy of Management journals) at the cost of diluting their disciplinary training. This makes sense given the recognition and reward strategies obtaining in institutions of management.

Also, there is the issue of internal disciplinary hierarchy within the field of management education with 'economists and finance specialists', for example, often viewing themselves 'as purveyors of solid, quantifiable data, and far superior to their colleagues' in other departments (Zald 2002: 372). So, the issue is not about some kind of conspiratorial downgrading of a social science discipline like sociology in management education, but the larger dynamics affecting the fortunes of academic disciplines across time periods and generations. In what follows, we try to outline a framework to help contextualise the relationship of sociology and management education in historical and contemporary terms.

The framework

A continual process of fission and fusion of academic disciplines has been a constant feature of the higher education landscape. The historical origins and contemporary status of management studies itself is the outcome of a selective fusion of certain aspects of the already established social and decision sciences. Likewise, the history of modern higher education has no scarcity of academic disciplines that emerged out of the fission of previously existing ones. Indeed, an academic discipline is a response to both – the pragmatic academic issues and wider political concerns that arise at a particular point in time in the history of a given society. Disciplines, as competing groupings of teachers and researchers, once institutionalised become distinctive social entities. However, their characteristic methods and concepts change over time in response to both internal and external conditions. Seen thus, the particular pattern of disciplinary differentiation is a function of the organisation and distribution of scientific labour at a particular point in time in a particular society. This pattern of labour embodies the negotiated outcome of a particular balance of power among socially organised academics where each discipline lays claim to its particular intellectual territory (Scott 2005: 15). Arguably, disciplinary distinctions are rarely based on coherent and logical divisions within systems of knowledge, making a 'scientific' advancement over earlier forms of understanding. According to Pierre Bourdieu (1996), they should be looked at as historically contingent products of the development of educational systems (habitus) within particular national contexts (fields). That probably explains why in France, the institution of *Grandes Ecoles* carried greater intellectual-academic weight than that of a research university or that a discipline like philosophy had unparalleled public esteem in France and Germany as compared to other countries. However, in most places that came under the sway of modern education, 'liberal arts and sciences were the historical core of the university', and 'formed the basis of the institutions' public recognition' for being the largest division in terms of faculty size and student enrolment (Machlup 1982: 151). The evolution of such academic disciplines and knowledge systems was rarely determined by the idea of truth alone. A sociology of knowledge and profession framework brings home the point that the existing or emerging constellation of social interests equally shapes knowledge paradigms and the system of academic disciplines. The power of money has no less a say in this evolution as we have seen its role in the early legitimisation of management as a university discipline. For instance, in the United States, in the early years of its origins, 'private benefactors, who had acquired their wealth from mercantile enterprise, were prepared to endow educational institutions disseminating practical knowledge for use in industry and trade' (Machlup 1982: 136).

Very often, an academic discipline is the outcome of a contested dialogue within the academy and also a response to larger social, political, and economic transformations. This is particularly true of social sciences. As Zald (2002: 372) notes, 'social science emerges as part of an epistemological and methodological discourse and debate in the academy, but also responds to demands for information in the larger society to changes in societal discourse'. Viewed thus, an academic discipline has two major components: an intellectual component, that is, 'the forms and kinds of knowledge and values the discipline wants to enhance', and an occupational component, that is, 'the ideology, organization, and command of resources, including status that the collective uses in order to justify and enhance itself in the academic and larger community'. These two interrelated aspects – the intellectual and the occupational – constitute the overall disciplinary project facilitating its claims over public resources, institutional legitimacy, and societal support. The perceived usefulness and relevance of a discipline determines its prestige and collective valuation of its intellectual products. That is how every society evolves a differentiated distribution of prestige and status of an academic discipline and the attendant profession within the overall system of disciplines and professions. In the light of this framework, enunciated among others by Abbott (2001, 2002) and Zald (2002), this slim volume presents select aspects of the institutionalisation and transformation of the disciplines of sociology and management to examine the changing contours of their interface.

The growing body of work in the sociology of professions and the sociology of science and knowledge reminds us of the need to see academic disciplines as unstable compounds that go through a series of contingent transformations depending upon a wide range of factors (Machlup 1972, 1982; Abbott 1988; Collini 2012). Some of these factors emanate from the disciplines themselves as they alternate between longer periods of everyday puzzle-solving and short spells of paradigm shifts (Kuhn 1962). Others evolve in the process of a discipline's response to a host of emergent institutional, political, and societal factors that mark the unfolding of human civilisation. Such factors necessarily bring in the characteristics of the field of national intellectual production and the global division of academic labour. Besides, the relative power play among the neighbouring disciplines based on their reputational rankings in the marketplace and their perceived scientific rigour in academic terms feed into the historical evolution and contemporary configuration of different academic disciplines.

Also, there is the vexing question of the relationship between disciplinarity and interdisciplinarity. Academics appear to be divided into two apparently warring camps championing one or the other. For some observers, interdisciplinary work by virtue of being 'problem-driven', and 'problem-oriented' empirical work does not create enduring, self-reproducing communities the way pure academic disciplines do (Abbott 2001: 133). For them, disciplines retain hierarchy over applied interdisciplinary areas because disciplines are repositories of 'problem-portable' knowledge. As against this, 'an interdisciplinary field generates problem-based knowledge which remains insufficiently abstract to survive in competition with problem-portable knowledge' (Abbott 2001: 135).

In fact, Abbott puts forward a strong case for the superiority of conventional disciplines. For him, disciplines are home to original, transformative work that subsequently gets translated into applied fields. Seen thus, the conventional academic disciplines act as 'exporters' of knowledge, whereas an interdisciplinary field is an 'importer' arena of academic knowledge produced elsewhere. Such an understanding gives rise to a reputational order that accords primacy to the well-established academic disciplines as the originator and initiator of paradigm-changing transformative debates, which feed into a healthy development of the applied interdisciplinary fields. True, the interaction between the two is rarely a one-way traffic. The empirical findings and interpretive insights of the applied interdisciplinary fields are ploughed back into the primary field of pure disciplines, and the process continues. Nevertheless, there continues to be almost a never-ending debate in terms of binaries, such as pure and applied, disciplinary and interdisciplinary, exporter and importer disciplines with the implied hint that the first unit of these binaries having an inherently superior resonance.

However, in recent times, the norms of academic governance have undergone considerable transformation. There is an increasing reliance on quantitative forms of benchmarking where organisations or institutions are ranked against a set of norms defined around notions of efficiency, productivity, relevance, and impact. The number of publications in 'star' journals, the number of patents garnered, the volume of revenue earned through research projects, and other measurable parameters go into the making of league tables and ranks. For instance, in the UK, the Research Excellence Framework (REF), the successor to the Research Assessment Exercise (RAE), is the latest instrument of academic governance in higher education. In India too, there is the National Institutional Ranking Framework (NIRF). While interdisciplinary research is mentioned in these documents, these assessments too tend to be organised along disciplinary lines. Indeed, they do emphasise impact, thereby encouraging problem-solving and applied interdisciplinary work. Yet, given the prevailing discipline-based measurement systems in higher education, the interdisciplinary research often has a problematic status in such research assessment exercises.

Interdisciplinarity now has new advocates and novel constituencies, including the new systems of academic governance. The latter are seen as concrete manifestations of neoliberal discourse and practice exemplifying commercialisation of knowledge and eliding questions of politics of knowledge production (Collini 2012). Moreover, there is a flourishing discourse around 'mode 2' knowledge, that is, applied interdisciplinary knowledge not necessarily produced in the older sites, such as universities, public research laboratories, and the like, but in the new sites of private research foundations, corporate bodies, consultancies, marketing survey agencies, opinion polls enterprises. This 'mode 2' knowledge, for some, is more than the outcome of contemporary governance of knowledge. Rather, it needs to be seen in terms of its epistemological presumptions and benefits. It is necessitated because of the change in the epistemological understanding of the actors and their agency. It heralds positive transformations in forms of accountability and should not be reduced as the handiwork of new forms and structures of governance. Arguably, whereas critics consider calls for interdisciplinarity primarily as ideological features or symptoms of neoliberal managerial regimes pervading the system of higher education, enthusiasts find elements of novelty, innovation, and accountability in them (Balon and Holmwood 2019). Besides, there are some who stress the impossibility of intellectual work in neoliberal regimes (Davies 2005).

There is another angle to the criticism of the disciplinary claim to expertise, though. It stems from a general scepticism towards the feasibility of a bounded object domain. The structural and cultural diffuseness of an object domain makes the formulation of a traditional view of the discipline an uncertain enterprise. Changes being inevitable ontological processes, different forms of expertise, including the interdisciplinary one, are needed to produce an understanding of such changes. In any case, as some philosophers of science argue, the world increasingly becomes what can be known through science, which moreover takes a particular form: 'the so-called natural sciences and the human or social sciences, which are increasingly closely combined with one another to the point of confusion' (Boltanski 2011: 131). Thus, interdisciplinarity can be read as being clearly related to the 'political metaphysics underlying this form of domination' (Bolantski 2011: 131). In this reading, interdisciplinarity becomes a necessary tool to solve problems or deal with the complexity of the world owing to an apparently autonomous reality. Put it differently; there is no simple association between interdisciplinarity and neoliberalism as there is the diversity of claims made for the former (Cooper 2012: 85).

This brief detour into disciplinarity–interdisciplinarity is apposite to make sense of the field of management studies that began as an interdisciplinary field and has gradually graduated into an almost stand-alone academic discipline and into a distinct academic profession with all its trappings of associations, conferences, undergraduate textbooks, internal disputes, in-house journals, and the like. Given its peculiar birthmarks, management studies have been continually negotiating an ideal balance between the force and pull of academic respectability and the burden of relevance and application of its knowledge. In a way, it has had to cater to the demands of a double hierarchy: academic-scholarly and everyday-mundane. And, its quest for an ideal terrain to anchor itself, both as an academic discipline and an application-oriented profession, has been fraught with a periodic plea for a fundamental reorientation of its mandate and purpose, occasionally caused by specific events (for example, the U.S. subprime crisis of 2008–2009 was one such specific event). Such events pave the way for a serious questioning of the general discourse surrounding an academic discipline and 'undermine the legitimacy or normative penumbra of topics and provide impetus for the reorganisation of the field' (Zald 2002: 372).

The outcomes of such a questioning are shaped by institutional contexts as well. To be sure, the latter impinge on the intellectual operations and reproduction of scientific fields as embodied in the structure of academic disciplines. The stratification order of management education is not immune from such influences. On the one hand, management education is subject to external forces, emanating from the transnational field, that propel it towards homogenisation and competitive isomorphism in relation to interrelated demands of rankings and accreditation. On the other hand, the societal concurrence of its value and contributions in the national field gets reflected through state policies of higher education, the high demand, and the rigour of entrance to institutions of management education. Institutions like IIMs in India and *Tres Grandes Ecoles* – HEC, ESSEC, and ESCP – in France exemplify these trends.

The book

There is abundant literature on management education: its historical origins and contemporary status. Likewise, there is no scarcity of writings on the history and present practices of sociology as a discipline. However, barring a few scattered essays and reflective pieces, there is probably not much on the theme dealt with in this slim volume: the dynamic interplay between two cognate disciplines with differing claims to academic respectability and relevance. With the eye focused on the past disciplinary engagements and adding a hopeful look ahead in terms of a mutually enriching agenda, this book is neither a work in disciplinary history nor an exercise in epistemological exegesis. This is more like a stock-taking of the collective scholarly enterprise designated by such intelligible terms as sociology and management from the perspective of a critical insider. Without any all-consuming claims of reflexivity, it intends to explore relations between management education and sociology in the context of an array of institutional and scholarly practices. Deliberatively selective in its consideration of themes and issues, it does not purport to be a comprehensive review of either of the two disciplines. That is why it does not attempt any neat linear chronological narrative of the disciplinary evolution, growth, and development of sociology and management as academic disciplines. True, it is not steeped in historical amnesia either as it brings out the often recriminatory arguments levelled at management education by the established scholarly disciplines for its myopic, short-sighted, and ahistorical understanding of its vocation. In the same vein, it excavates select vignettes from sociology's disciplinary past to underline its utterly ambiguous scope and indeterminate substantive domain.

Diverse conceptualisations of these disciplinary areas notwithstanding, there have been unidirectional movements of sociologists from conventional universities to institutions of management bringing in its wake new institutional and professional configurations for both the disciplines. While for management the challenge is to draw upon sociological frameworks without losing its distinctiveness, the task for sociology is to demonstrate its relevance in an applied setting where it is not possible for a sociologist to talk of ideological state apparatuses or class character of the state, or the reproduction of inequality, or structure versus agency, or orthodoxy versus critique, or consensus versus conflict that can very well be done in a university classroom. This book is particularly oriented towards the peculiar demands that get generated when sociology and management education interact under the well-established institutional frameworks. In this sense, this book is neither sociology of management education nor about sociology in management education. As the title makes it amply clear, it is about sociology and management education: their engagements (past and present) and agendas (future).

The book consists of five chapters: an introduction, a conclusion, and three substantive chapters. The next chapter, 'Becoming a Science: The Quest for Academic Respectability', discusses the making of sociology and management as collective disciplinary projects. As Zald (2002) argues, the becoming a science model was chosen not only because of its innate intellectual attractiveness but because it facilitated their legitimation and status mobility in the larger academy. The becoming a science model carried with it a set of important pay-offs – public esteem, institutional recognition, and societal endorsement. The attainment of the becoming a science project remains incomplete, though, in both the cases. Sociology remains a low consensus pre-paradigmatic discipline despite its longer history of existence in the academy as compared

Introduction 11

to management. The latter continues to carry the historical burden of having been an importer interdisciplinary field despite its spectacular growth and unparalleled popularity.

Since both the disciplines are concerned with issues of the human world in its everyday institutional and organisational manifestations, their problem formulations transgress internal scholarly and disciplinary puzzles about fundamental and universal aspects of human life. Whereas sociology has sought to synthesise and integrate its varying approaches and theoretical frameworks within a unifying and coherent scheme, it has not been able to shed its image of a 'fractal' discipline (Abbott 2001). Management too is yet to gain the ultimate authority of a theoretically driven scholarly branch of knowledge in relation to its disciplinary others. However, both the disciplines have successfully achieved the status of scholarly coherence to an extent where they have control over their academic field's agenda. They very well provide disciplinary walls for their specialists to set their own research and teaching agendas. And, both are subject to the outside world of impact, relevance and applied knowledge, and new forms of academic governance. In a manner of speaking, both the disciplines remain committed to the credible empirical analysis of phenomena under investigation.

Chapter 3, Meandering Pathways: Betwixt the National and the Global, maps out the interactions between sociology and management education in the context of institutions of management in India. Drawing upon the disciplinary history of sociology in India, it discusses the nature and direction of rather a limited traffic between the two. It brings out the primacy of university as an institutional anchor of sociology, which has a particularly disabling effect on its dexterity to work in the applied interdisciplinary setting of an institution of management. The chapter details sociological practices in relation to management education and research. It also looks at the implications of foundational social science disciplines like sociology for the consolidation and transformation of management studies as a field. This chapter also brings into sharper relief the competing demands of national distinctiveness and conformity to global benchmarks and standards of excellence that management education has been subjected to. The chapter points out the dangers of a homogenising vision of management education that is likely to strengthen the already existing U.S. dominance in the field.

'Privileging Critique: Sociology and Its Metamorphosis into Critical Management Studies', is the title of the next chapter, which critically examines the emergent field of Critical Management Studies (CMS).

CMS emerged as an ideological critique of the underlying values of rationalisation and efficiency that informed conventional management studies and is known for its 'commitment to deconstructive methodologies and the whole concern for representation and signification' (Zald 2002: 375). CMS is a curious mixture of left politics, critical theory, Marxism, and post-modern epistemologies. In the words of Zald (2002: 376), CMS is some kind of conjunction of 'left ideology and methodologies derived from hermeneutics and deconstruction'. What distinguishes CMS from a long history of the left-inspired critique of business corporations and modern management is its post-modern sensibility. Even as the CMS academics are 'mostly in the less core departments of schools of management (less core as seen by both students and by senior administrators and external elites)', they have been largely successful in creating a buzz around the novelty of CMS. As Zald (2002: 378) notes, 'most business school faculty who identify themselves with CMS are located in organisational behaviour or management departments, with a sprinkling in accounting, computer and information systems, international business and other units, very few are in marketing and none in finance'. In effect, organisational behaviour is the main institutional habitat for CMS as it concerns the larger socio-political context and interpersonal relations for its investigation into organisational culture, design, and structure. Given this focus, organisational behaviour recruits few sociologists and more psychologists. And, it is they who are the flag bearers of CMS. CMS mounts its attention on the dark side of global capitalism. Its focus goes beyond the profit concerns of a business firm and encompasses larger intersections that make the market work: trust, institutions, regulations, moral and ethical values, and ideological and political choices and claims. This chapter offers a critique of CMS as well and outlines its possible futures in the context of its uncomfortable relationship with its institutional surroundings.

While delineating the relationship between sociology and management education, this book takes cognisance of the larger institutional arrangements and stratification system of disciplines. The book will appeal to students of sociology, management, educational administrators, and general students of higher education. After all, sociology has been an inalienable part of management education ever since the latter started fashioning its self-image as a rigorous academic discipline drawn from the hitherto existing social and mathematical sciences. Besides a general mapping of the intersections and engagements between sociology and management education, the book looks at the specific context of India and the nature and direction of disciplinary traffic in terms of both teaching and research between sociology and management. It examines the distinctive characteristics of these interactions in the wider context of global management education. The book reveals an acute awareness of the dominance of the U.S. model in the field and the general clamour for its emulation across the globe. While employing a perspective from the Global South, it contextualises the discussion in relation to the wider geopolitics of knowledge production.

It does present an agenda of a promising prospective engagement between the two disciplines and lays down some of the ways in which such an engagement can be made mutually enriching. In an implicit way, the book contains an assessment of Indian scholarly contributions to the fields of sociology and management education and lays bare some of the processes and factors that characterise our continued reliance on American/Western theoretical models, frameworks, and constructs. CMS has surely done a commendable job in questioning and critiquing the underlying foundational premises of management education. It is an encouraging sign that Indian scholars, too, are joining this critical endeavour. That day should not be far off when India ceases to mere providers of local empirical material and cases for the construction of theoretical apparatuses in the Global North.

2 Becoming a science
The quest for academic respectability

The history of sociology and management studies has been characterised by their shared desire to gain scientific status and the attendant academic respectability. This chapter brings out the aspects of this intertwined history to shed light on their present status and identity. In the initial phase of their disciplinary consolidation, both the disciplines struggled for institutional and professional legitimacy to establish themselves as scholarly branches of knowledge. Against this backdrop, the chapter outlines the real and potential interactions between sociology and management studies.

The modern academy has been the chief arbiter of the academic respectability of an emergent discipline. By including a discipline in its institutional structure of faculties and departments, a university ends up according public recognition and institutional legitimacy to the scientific (scholarly) status of a discipline. Subsequently, such a recognised discipline starts developing its own protocols of an identifiable and (more or less) distinct disciplinary identity: professional associations, journals, conferences, textbooks, readers, anthologies, and resource books, standard curriculum, and syllabi, distinctive theoretical and methodological approaches, and, most importantly, an exclusive subject matter for investigation and study. Modern social sciences too have gone through similar processes of (mostly) fission whereby earlier umbrella categories of moral philosophy and political economy gave rise to disciplines such as economics, law, political science, sociology, and psychology through endless re-organisation of faculties and departments in the modern university system (Machlup 1972, 1982).

However, the formation of a new academic discipline has hardly ever been a smooth affair. More often than not, a new academic discipline has to face the resistance of the previously established ones and has to argue its case in terms of either the novelty of the subject matter,

DOI: 10.4324/9781003257813-2

or the ingenuity of perspective, or a combination of the extant (dominant) attributes which go into the making of its scholarly distinctiveness. These processes have frequently been time-consuming and have witnessed much acrimonious debate among the professoriate and the self-declared custodians of science and scholarship. History of sociology testifies to these struggles wherein Emile Durkheim (1858–1917), one of sociology's founding fathers, had to make a case for sociological 'method' and 'social fact' against the then dominance of the psychological (Durkheim 1982). As against the processes of fission, some disciplines are the outcomes of selective processes of fusion. Management is one of them; environmental studies, international relations, biotechnology, science and technology studies, genetic engineering can be cited as other examples.

Even as all academic disciplines aspire to possess all the possible attributes of distinctiveness, their actual accomplishments vary considerably. Disciplines like sociology which find themselves saddled with a wobbly subject matter 'social' (too all-encompassing to lend itself to the sharp drawing of the disciplinary boundary) insist on the primacy of their theoretical and methodological distinctiveness than on the neatness of their subject matter. Even otherwise, a discipline's exclusive claim over its 'object' of investigation is frequently contested. Surprisingly, economics, the *prima donna* of modern social sciences, too finds its object – the economy – occasionally contested by political economists and economic sociologists. It is a different matter altogether that economics has successfully marginalised its potential competitors by its robust institutional gate-keeping (the status deficit concerning those who do economic history or political economy, and their frequent institutional location in non-mainstream economics departments, is a case in point).

By contrast, sociology could not have this historical privilege of a well-demarcated object. As a consequence, sociology has remained some kind of a broad and unstable tent. Past attempts (those of the American sociologist Talcott Parsons' being the most significant) to impose theoretical and methodological order and coherence on the discipline have miserably failed. Moreover, sociology has never really reached a workable consensus on what its object is: '"society", "social facts", "social action" were the classical options, with the list growing over time to include social networks, rational action, actor networks, etc.' (Scott 2020: 444).

Yet, disciplinarity can very well be seen as a way of ordering reality. As Scott (2020: 444) puts it elegantly, 'disciplines make a "finite cut" from "meaningless infinity" to create "walls" behind which "deep specialization" could be fostered and protected'. According to him, disciplines have come to act as "defences" so that very often, the loss of a disciplinary anchor does pose dilemmas to a modern-day scholar. Without such an anchor, she feels lost when it comes to negotiating rival disciplinary claims over the object of her investigation. Equally, she is lost as to the source of methodological and theoretical coherence for her study and research. In this sense, an academic discipline is not merely a boundary-demarcating mechanism but also the foundation of intellectual socialisation in the distinct logics of a branch of knowledge. At the same time, disciplines are also the constituents of the rank-ordering of different branches of learning that generate a given hierarchy of disciplines at a given point in time. Historically speaking, a discipline's distance from practice has granted it a relatively higher status (Ramnath 2017). For a long time, the historically transmitted academic hierarchical systems have drawn on the binaries of pure and applied research, theoretical and empirical research, wherein the pure and theoretical have trumped applied and empirical. These distinctions are dynamic, though.

In recent times, amidst the incessant talk of inter-disciplinarity and the government-driven emphasis on relevance and impact, such old binaries may not carry the same significance. The shifting opportunity structures in the marketplace have created new and legitimising rationale for the applied and interdisciplinary research. In contemporary literature, there is the celebration of *Mode 2* research as against the earlier type of *Mode 1* research (university-based pure, theoretical without much concern for relevance and impact).

An academic discipline, once institutionalised, becomes a self-contained and self-reproducing enterprise. Indeed, its subsequent growth and development do not play out by the logics of the academy alone in which it seeks to establish its scholarly reputation. The distinctiveness of national contexts and knowledge traditions do play a role.

That is why there remains a degree of national-geographical variability of the hierarchy of the disciplines even when the broad contours remain the same. For instance, in no other country, a sociologist has enjoyed the type of professional prestige as has been bestowed on them in the United States. Likewise, philosophers in France outweigh social scientists in terms of their reputation as public intellectuals. Economists have enjoyed unparalleled prestige in the United Kingdom in relation to France. Germany has been less receptive to management as a discipline compared to other European countries. Viewed thus, the conflicting imperatives of outside stakeholders (the nation-state being the pre-eminent one) have historically impinged on the academy and have influenced its sense of the hierarchical arrangement of disciplines (Scott 2020: 444).

In the remainder of this chapter, we outline the evolving disciplinary identities of sociology and management in the modern academy. We also examine their historical interface in the making of modern-day management education.

Sociology and its discontents

Sociologists have often lamented the pre-paradigmatic status of their discipline. Moreover, they have equally been uneasy about the intellectual expanse that their discipline has historically stood for. True, sociology has its classics and other canonical texts of its founding fathers to keep up the pretence of a certain sociological core. However, its core has perpetually been in a state of coming apart given the unwieldy breadth of sociology's subject matter. For the most part, it has served as a vast heterogeneous enterprise whose ecumenical width has precluded either the fostering of a sharp analytical edge or any cumulative congealing of theoretical knowledge. It lacks the type of a 'general theory', for example, found in economics that synthesises its historical disciplinary legacy or the accumulated stock of knowledge. There is no indivisible disciplinary heritage available to its practitioners. In fact, there is no working understanding on any list of 'core concepts' that constitute the discipline. The only consensus about the disciplinary core is its continuing dissensus about the elements of that core. The cognitive pendulum swings from one extreme of its conceptualisation as an art form *a la* Robert Nisbet's "unit ideas" to Talcott Parsons' audaciously ambitious attempt to propound a general scientific theory of social system in terms of the latter's enunciation of pattern variables. Alan Scott (2020) is not off the mark when he claims that it is well-night impossible to talk of 'heterodox sociology' (the way we speak of 'heterodox economics', for instance) precisely because we do not know as to what 'orthodoxy', or 'mainstream', stands for in sociology.

According to Goran Therborn (2000: 47–57), sociology has undoubtedly been a rich country. It has ceaselessly held conversations with disciplines both near and far: political science, economics, literary studies, philosophy, social work, history, psychology. The list is, indeed, a long one. This has prompted Holmwood (2010) to pronounce that inherent inter-disciplinarity has been one of the foundational attributes of sociology as an academic discipline. One of the outcomes of such a wide range of conversations has been the indistinct projection of its disciplinary subject matter, that is, the project of studying 'the social', or 'society'. These very terms reveal as if the whole human social ecumene had been claimed as legitimate for sociological investigation. The attempts of successive generations of sociologists have hardly yielded a workable delimitation of this wide sociological outlook into anything remotely resembling a paradigm. As noted earlier, Talcott Parsons did attempt at creating a neoclassical sociology, roughly coeval with the successful neo-classical syntheses in economics, but to no avail. On the contrary, its recent history is more like the uncoupling of a hitherto loosely held and an over-stretched discipline whereby its gigantic 'core' (if ever there was one!) has been and is being sliced into separate territories of cognition, adding further to its unmanageable diversity, and in a way, impeding any effective coagulation and accumulation, and thereby the very reproduction of the discipline (Holmwood 2014).

Therborn (2000:52) justifiably refers to what he calls the Lecturer's Dilemma in a non-paradigmatic discipline like sociology: 'how to teach an intellectual sprawl, such as actually existing sociology?' There have been several pragmatic responses to this dilemma. Some sociologists have taken recourse to an overview of social institutions and social categories studied by sociologists and base and communicate their disciplinary understanding accordingly. Some others have tried to present sociology through a set of illustrious predecessors and their schools of thought, 'isms' so to say. In Therborn's (2000:52) reading, the British sociologist Anthony Giddens belongs to the former category, whereas the American sociologist Randall Collins can be seen as belonging to the latter.

However, the most frequent recourse has been to underplay the distinctiveness of its subject matter and to hide behind the distinctiveness of sociological perspective/approach/imagination/sensibility. The Indian sociologist M. N. Srinivas (1994: 12) thus highlights sociology's uniqueness in relation to an *approach* and a *perspective* that it brings to bear on every aspect of society and culture that it studies. This compensates for the fact that sociology, unlike other social sciences, does not have a clearly demarcated field of its own. Thus, for Srinivas, a sociological approach enables students of society to 'try and look at society as a whole, and see the various parts or institutions in relation to each other, and to the whole'. Another well-known American sociologist Peter L. Berger (1992), adds a triumphalist note to this usual rationale frequently resorted to by the practitioners of sociology when he asserts that the *sociological perspective* has entered into the cognitive instrumentarium of most of the human sciences with great success. According to him, sociologists, unlike most other social scientists, mostly offer their *perspective* on a wide range of empirical phenomena. It is not for nothing that most historians have somewhere incorporated the sociological perspective into their work. In a related vein, one needs to barely mention the American sociologist C. Wright Mills whose 1959 title *The Sociological Imagination* has provided oft-quoted mantras to generations of sociologists ever since to articulate a sense of their professional identity and disciplinary distinctiveness.

Be that as it may, by the last quarter of the nineteenth century, sociology had successfully entered the bolt-holes of the modern professional system as a university-sanctified discipline. The first university department of sociology (and anthropology) had been established at the University of Chicago in 1893. The first professional journal – the *American Journal of Sociology* – had started its publication in 1895; slightly later than the *American Journal of Psychology* (1887), way earlier than *American Journal of Economics* (1911), and much earlier than the *Academy of Management Journal* (1958). Likewise, Emile Durkheim had already started teaching sociology at the University of Bordeaux in 1887 and played a key role in the institutionalisation of sociology in France in the 1890s, both through his influential works like *The Division of Labour in Society* (1893), *The Rules of Sociological Method* (1895), and *Suicide* (1897), and more importantly, through the founding of sociological periodicals, *Revue Internationale de Sociologie* (1893) and *L'Année Sociologique* (1898). Anthony King (2007: 504) justifiably remarks, 'In Germany, France, and the United States, by contrast, sociology enjoyed high academic status from the beginning of the twentieth century'.[1] His comparison is to the case of the United Kingdom where L. T. Hobhouse occupied the first chair of sociology in 1909, and where there has been relatively weak professional development.

History apart, disciplinary developments, and concomitantly, a discipline's changing fortunes in relation to public esteem and institutional legitimacy are shaped by both a discipline's internal tendencies in the course of its evolution and the changes in external conditions such as governance structures of higher education, public funding, the introduction of audit culture and new forms of public accountability, as well as the focus on impact, relevance and usefulness of knowledge. As far as the internal tendencies go, sociology has had rather weak monopolistic claims over its subject matter. Not surprisingly, sociology has been very productive in spawning new disciplinary fields and has historically acted as an 'exporter' discipline to fields such as management, criminology, social policy, education, international relations, area studies and science and technology studies (Holmwood 2010, 2011; Balon and Holmwood 2019). In fact, over the years, we have seen the emergence and growth of different sociologies without much interaction among them, and certainly without any significant efforts to find a shared common basis or synthesis that would reduce their plurality and diversity of knowledge claims. This is why Abbott (2001) calls sociology an academic field of high 'fractal' dimension whose diverse knowledges not only cannot be integrated but also are in a perpetual state of mutual opposition and even denial. In his evocative phrase, sociology appeared as a 'caravansary on the Silk Road'.

Moreover, sociology remained inhabited by 'bandit gangs of positivists, feminist, interactionist and Marxists' (Abbott, 2001: 6). In his reading, sociology as a discipline then turns out to be an inventory of mutually incompatible and inconsistent approaches. Thus, a certain 'laissez-faire' approach to explanatory problems became an inherent disciplinary attribute giving rise to disjunctions and discrepancies in the scholarly field. These chaotic origins of sociology have to do with the fact that there is 'no kind of work about society that could be demonstrated to be not-sociology' (Abbott 2001: 144). In other words, historically speaking, there has been no area specific to sociology. By contrast, all areas which sociologists have engaged with are the ones where sociology's disciplinary others can lay legitimate coparcenary knowledge claims. Even institutions like family and marriage, long held to be quintessential institutions for sociological research, have attracted the scholarly interest of economists.

Thus, its constitutive features themselves have rendered sociology an almost impossible scientific discipline (Balon and Holmwood 2019: 333–47). Its eclecticism has been its main undoing for its status as a science. Its considered view that everything about society is the legitimate object of sociology (sanctified by past masters whose overweening ambition was to fashion sociology as an imperial discipline right at the top of social science hierarchy under the Comptean inspiration of positive science) has imparted it a weak disciplinary identity right from its birth. It could not develop a distinctive methodology of its own. Nor could it possess the analytical acuity and agility of more methodologically oriented disciplines like economics and psychology. It kept humming the song of the disparate nature of the social to endlessly justify its indistinct epistemological and ontological pronouncements. No wonder, sociology could not constitute itself as a science and, for many, remained an ideology despite few attempted systematisation of its knowledge under the positivist influence of structural-functionalism.

As a matter of fact, the different sociologies have been frequently terming other sociologies as misconceived or 'impossible'. For a long, Marxist sociologists called much of sociology as an embodiment of bourgeois status-quoism, and not proper science. Ethno-methodologists found sociology wanting as a proper science notwithstanding its 'systematic' empiricism (Balon and Holmwood 2019: 333–47). Some others find sociology a residual discipline despite its claims to the contrary. According to Jurgen Habermas (1984: 4), 'sociology originated as discipline responsible for the problems that politics and economics pushed to one side on their way to becoming specialized sciences'. As John Holmwood (2010, 2011) emphatically reminds us, sociology carries within itself a certain critical inter-disciplinarity which has historically marked its fragile existence as an exporter discipline. This inherent inter-disciplinarity has cast sociology in the mold of an unsettled intellectual territory. And, because sociology itself does not have a 'settled' character and because sociology's disciplinary identity is strongly associated with inter-disciplinarity, it has failed to make a mark as a strong social science of value and significance. As Andrew Abbott (2001: 3) remarks, sociology 'is also the most general of the social sciences, or, to put it less politely, the least defined'.

This greater generality of sociology makes it particularly vulnerable to annexation by other disciplines as well as from other interdisciplinary subject areas. It does not have the solid disciplinary self-identity like economics and political science to stand its scholarly ground without being lost in the residual problems of other disciplines (Holmwood 2010). Given its peculiar history, sociology has become 'a discipline of many topics'. It has always been acquiring them and seldom letting them go. 'Sociology, in short, is irredeemably interstitial. In fact, this interstitiality is what undergirds sociology's claims as a general social science, claims not necessarily justified by its contributions in theory, method, or substance' (Abbott 2001: 6). As we will see in Chapter 3, most of the Critical Management Studies (CMS) scholars have come to celebrate this imprecise and the most general nature of sociology as a sign of its polycentrism, criticality, and openness to new voices and social constituencies, to oppositional movements, and whatnot.

In effect, sociology is the target of principally two types of attacks. There is one stream of thought that questions the very possibility of a science of society or the social on philosophical grounds based on its particular conceptualisation of what sciences are or should be. There is the second line of thought that does not negate the possibility of a social science but does not consider sociology equipped enough to

22 Becoming a science

fit the bill as a candidate social science. For example, an influential sociologist Peter Winch (1958), belongs to the former. He simply does not entertain any possibility of a science of social relations. For him, a scientific sociology is well-nigh impossible because the available models of science themselves are deficient and faulty. He avers, 'the central problem of sociology, that of giving an account of the nature of social phenomena in general, itself belongs to philosophy' (Winch, 1958: 43). In his reading, rather than constituting itself as a branch of science, sociology should be understood as an adjunct of philosophy. Louch (1963), on the other hand, does not negate the idea of social science as such but has reservations about the status of sociology as a candidate social science. He has serious discomfort with the very conduct of sociology as an empirical enterprise. According to him, sociology 'embraces a group of questions and subjects so loosely connected that it would be mistaken to speak of, and idle to project, a procedure common to all of them' (Louch 1963: 273). Balon and Holmwood (2019: 335) present a range of such internal and external critique of sociology arising out of what they call its 'weak identification with a disciplinary core, whether methodological, as would be typical in the case of anthropology and the role of ethnography, or analytical, as in the case of economics and psychology'.

Even those who otherwise do not disagree with sociology's claim to the 'social' as an object of scientific inquiry, think that the proper object of inquiry is the behaviours (actions) of individuals. According to Balon and Holmwood (2019: 335), sociology has frequently been put on the defensive by such criticisms. These criticisms undermine the long-cherished received wisdom of sociologists passed down by masters like Durkheim (1982) and Parsons (1937), who taught us to regard the 'social' as more than the sum total of individual actions. Generations of sociologists used to seeing the 'social' in terms of emergent properties, or as a *sui generis* reality, are evidently in for a rude shock when they come across Latour's argument that the 'social' is not an explanatory category as it is founded on the unsustainable binary distinctions between nature and society, and non-humans and human (Latour 2004).

Likewise, most of the constitutive categories of sociology have been attacked by the group of post-modern and post-structuralist scholars as furthering the grand narratives of science, history, truth, enlightenment rationality and the triumphalist modernity. In their collective celebration of the 'fragments', categories like 'social' themselves are rendered suspect. These new zealots find 'the social' as a problematic explanatory framework employed by sociologists because it smacks of what they reject as positivism and empiricism based on an inherently deficient understanding of modern science. Before aiming for a science of society, they enjoin us to adequately understand the nature of science on ontological grounds (that is, the nature of the objects of social science) and on epistemological grounds (that is, the nature of valid knowledge claims). In other words, as Holmwood (2011) asserts, sociology is to be developed, in the first instance, via the philosophy of science. For a discipline, torn apart by the irreconcilable ambition and promise of combining science and social criticism under the same roof, the post-modernist 'cultural' turn has further compounded its plurality.

And, commentators have increasingly noted its wide range of ailments and deficiencies. The perpetual diagnosis of all its ills is very often taken to be a sign of its robustness as a reflexive discipline and also evidence enough of its being with the most introspective discipline among the social sciences (Savage 2010: 659). This could though very well be a poor consolation for the practitioners of sociology when confronted with an inexhaustible list of ailments. Inglis (2014: 100) presents the list with a certain brevity for the UK context which can be extended to the general state of sociology. According to him, sociology is seen as ... being seriously underpowered in terms of quantitative methodological expertise ...; being entranced by superficial, 'cultural studies' sorts of concerns ... being an 'exporter discipline' – providing personnel to neighbouring disciplines like management studies – which is in danger of losing its own distinct identity ...; being in thrall to empirically unsubstantiated 'social theory'...; and being in need of radical methodological overhaul, away from older concerns to do with causality towards newer concerns to do with 'surface level' social phenomena ....

Evidently, the overall picture that emerges is of sociology being a softer qualitative discipline with undesirable eclecticism marking its historical legacy. This surely puts sociology in an inferior position to more quantitative and hence 'scientific' disciplines parading their ware in the institutional landscape of management education. Sociology comes with other disadvantages as well. Much of what it deals with in terms of subject matter is something that students have either heard of (about) or experienced themselves by virtue of their being members of a given society. Naturally, they have a propensity to write off sociology as something they already knew/know based on their common sense, or need not make rigorous efforts to learn it. This builds up the gradual public disregard for sociology as an academic discipline of lesser provenance, not a real science of consequence. Moreover, sociology offers no unambiguous and definitive answer to a problem that management students are prone to look for. The answers it provides are too broad to give quick-fix, relevant and effective insights into real-life business problems.

Such broad conceptualisations of sociology have interestingly come to inform not only its self-image but also the justifications it provides for its relevance to management education. Some of the arguments would typically run as follows. Business is fundamentally about people and their interactions. And people are not the same all through and their differences render the today's business environment different from yesterdays. Thus, in order to understand the dynamism of the business environment, in our teaching, we need to impart a more sociological approach to business. Sociology gives us deep scholarship, thereby allowing for a better understanding of complex social and economic challenges. Sociology, with its focus on groups, organisations and human interaction is a natural complement to business and industry. It enriches a business person's ability to manage these relations. To excel in business, one needs more than a solid grasp of mathematics and economics. One essentially requires an understanding of people, large populations in particular. Given that sociology is the scientific study of society including patterns of social relationship, social interaction, and culture, it helps one understand the complex relationships between nations (geo-politics) as well as within the multinational corporations. Actual business transactions happen between people and sociology gives one a good understanding of human behaviour.

In other words, sociology imparts skills that come in handy while researching the market conditions, trying to improve products/services, or boosting the morale of one's team. Sociology helps one move forward in a world of different cultures, genders, religions, and sexualities. It helps one in dealing with the employees in the workplace as one understands the cultural and social aspects that shape the behaviour of a team member. Sociology aids analytical thinking in relation to qualitative and quantitative data as one figures out how a multiplicity of social and cultural factors affect a population or shape their taste and preferences. For some, the rapidly changing business world, globalisation, technological innovation, and diversity in the workplace all require use of the sociological imagination. Then, knowledge about people's culture, buying habits, income levels, and the quality of life as a whole requires sociological understanding in terms of customers' economic and cultural background.

Put it differently, sociology can potentially contribute to marketing research. Sociology also gives an understanding of macro-phenomena that influence groups of people such as civil war, ethnic strife, nationalist jingoism, etc. That is to say, sociology can be a useful tool for country risk analysis for the purposes of investment and setting up a business. In any case, a business relationship is an interactive exchange between two organisations embedded in a network of business connections, so it is imperative to understand the social dimensions of business relations. A sociological perspective offers a critical lens to view society and thereby facilitates critical thinking regarding complex challenges facing a given society and also a better understanding of business outcomes and market opportunities. And lastly, sociology can contribute to the employment of better public relations by management as it helps them know better the target audience's cultural beliefs, religious practices, and surrounding values. The ultimate stock justification has been something like this: since business is about organisations and people, social forces shaping the workplace, organisation structures, and the economy; it is important to employ sociological understanding to have a critical understanding of the broader societal processes and forces (Brown and Harrison 1980; Hauser 1961; Kohout 1968; Linstead 1984; Joseph 1991; Mandjak and Sazanto 2010).

At all events, sociology, as such, has not been stranger to the curriculum of the American schools of business and management, a state of affairs which reflects the high standing of sociology in that country and the strategic importance of Elton Mayo's appointment at the Harvard Business School.[2] Way back in 1960, Smith (1960: 103) could claim that 'Indeed, the position of sociology in business and management education in the United States now seems to be such that it has passed beyond the point at which separate reference needs to be made to it in the curriculum'. True, even in the School of Industrial Management at the MIT, sociology was present more by way of immersing its separate identity in the interdisciplinary theme areas. Nevertheless, the available evidence suggests that the relevance of things sociological to management process has been taken for granted, at least in the United States, and also to a large extent in the United Kingdom.

In fact, very often, the case for inclusion of sociology in management curriculum has largely been made on the basis of its achievement in the United States where the contributions of Elton Mayo looms large. On the flip side, it has also meant equating industrial sociology with Hawthorne experiments. As a consequence, sociology is looked at as a palliative for industrial conflict and a source of 'social skills' – it has been seen as contributing to solving human (read labour) problems in the industrial societies. In this fashion, sociology justified its limited uses in business schools and/or in management teaching. In the

United Kingdom, sociology has been projected as being essentially a study of institutions including a description of representative industrial institutions – the enterprise, the trade union, and the labour market. Besides, it included in its provenance the concept of formal and informal behaviour at work place and focussed on the interaction of industrial with other institutions of society-those of class, politics, and education. In a manner of speaking, by providing illustrative material on industrial situations, the industrial problems, and their social implications, sociology has managed to sneak in through the backdoor of business schools.

On another plane, as noted earlier, sociology has also resorted to the general and oft-repeated justification of its being a liberalising influence on aspiring managers and contributing to the understanding of the world manager lives and works. Sociology helps students become more conscious of the subtleties of social environment and the processes of social change shaping it. It is useful in the sense that sociology offers clues into the behaviour of employees as the latter is linked to social structure as a whole. The general argument has been that sociological knowledge makes management students alive to the long-term changes affecting their world. It is equally useful as the managers get insights into the varieties of human values and conduct which sharpen their understanding of the social context. The overall claim runs like this: sociology can teach managers something about the social structure of industrial institutions, the social values which sustain them, and the social context in which they function; and that the teaching of this kind is both a liberal element in that it broadens the perspective of the student, and at the same time, a useful one, in that it gives him knowledge which may be relevant to practical decisions (Smith 1960: 108).

Management as an academic field: between relevance and rigour

More than a century after its origins as primarily a vocational programme of training to practising managers, there is little real consensus about what management education is all about and what it actually entails. It is neither unnecessary provocation nor undue exaggeration to assert that management education is what effectively takes place in the business schools. The very fact that business schools have turned out to be commonly used shorthand term for an institute/school of management is revealing enough. On the one hand, such a usage privileges the modern corporation (and, in turn, the shareholders' firm) as the pre-eminent business entity; on the other, it reinforces the reigning American understanding of what management education is, or ought to be. There is an abundant literature delineating the idea of management education and the practices of business schools. This literature does have its fair share of periodically expressed existential angst about the direction management education has taken and the course correction it needs to do. Such angst gets more pronounced whenever there is a major crisis in the global corporate world. For example, the subprime crisis of 2008–2009 generated fervent pleas for imbuing management education with the lofty ideals of ethics, social responsibility, and sustainability. It led to major calls for the revamping of management curriculum and sustained introspection on the part of major players in the field pertaining to their larger role in society.

In this section, we present a synoptic review of the growth and development of management as an academic discipline in relation to its global institutional expansion. This review is primarily meant to underline the yet unsettled status anxiety of management studies as an academic discipline. It attempts to highlight the ambiguities and tensions that have marked the field regarding its proper realm of belonging – the academia or the world of practitioners.

Indeed, for much of the twentieth century, management education occupied a subordinate position in the academic pantheon and was much looked down upon by older and more established subject areas. Conventionally speaking, the credit for uplifting the academic status of management education goes to Taylor's *The Principles of Scientific Management* (1911). This book singlehandedly created the image of management being a mathematical, logical, engineering-like, rational, and even a scientific discipline. As the progenitor of scientific management, Taylor introduced two forms of division of labour inside companies: the first is his classical (horizontal) division of work into minute work tasks, and the second is his vertical division placing this knowledge firmly into the hands of those who now organise and manage the manufacturing process, that is, management. To many observers, Taylor's 'scientific management' reads like a despicable ideology, especially when he writes sentences like 'a worker is too stupid properly to train himself', [and that a worker] shall be so stupid and so phlegmatic that he [...] resembles [the] mental make-up of the ox [and that a worker must be kept] so stupid that the word "percentage" has no meaning to him [and finally workers are so stupid that even a] gorilla [can] become a more efficient pig-iron handler than any man can be (Taylor, 1911: 23, 21, 14 cited in Klikauer 2018: 453–62). Even now, though much criticised, his work remains a founding text of management which was successful in imparting management with a much-needed prefix – scientific. Howsoever ideological, it achieved at one single stroke the continuing belief in management's superiority over workers (seen as ox, and gorilla). As management education expanded institutionally and prospered, people teaching there began to feel that they deserved to be accorded higher status, and especially a greater degree of recognition from their peers. When refugees from declining disciplines such as sociology joined business schools in the 1980s and 1990s, the demand for respect became even stronger. The key underlying desire was to demonstrate that business and management were proper subjects in their own right, with relevant theory and rigorous methodologies. The upshot was an increasing willingness to mimic the natural sciences – to copy the approach of those subjects which were considered unimpeachable in terms of their seriousness about creating real scientific knowledge. Greater emphasis on quantification and empirical positivism followed. Business school faculty at long last could write proper papers like natural sciences with a standard academic format – literature review, methods and data, findings and discussion, summary and conclusion. Academic respectability was gained. In the process, other traditions were side-lined; for example, qualitative investigations into messy but real human life situations were considered inferior or subjective meanderings and hence non-scientific (Starkey and Tiratsoo 2007: 131–2).

Noticeably, the status of management education has been incredibly linked with the changing idea of what a university stands for. For a long, the university has been taken to be the pre-eminent site for the production of new knowledge. An academic discipline entering the portals of a university meant that the discipline has acquired some kind of consensual intellectual/scientific patina. Given the long-prevalent university protocols of according scientific/academic status to a discipline, management education had to struggle hard to get the type of academic esteem that other university disciplines enjoyed. Of course, it not only succeeded in gaining that respectability but also has successfully rendered some other previously established disciplines insecure through its sheer popularity and command of resources. In retrospect, one could even say that it was a kind of foolish conceit on the part of the custodians of the established disciplines and the grand idea of a university to assume that the existing zeitgeist would remain unaltered forever. The glamorous success of management education has altered that zeitgeist forever. In fact, it is the classic case of turning the tables.

There was a time when an established academic discipline like sociology looked down upon management as an upstart field meant for ambitious young people solely interested in MBAs as a quick and painless shortcut to upward professional mobility. People in the field of management were seen as those possibly interested in enjoying the material rewards that it guarantees than concerned with deeper questions of scholarship or the creation and dissemination of new knowledge. This thinking largely mirrored then prevailing ideological currents in the world around them. We appear to have come full circle now. Now, the previously established academic disciplines seek to allay their insecurities and project their new-found legitimacy and relevance by parading the real and potential contributions that they have made to MBA as a programme in particular and the field of management education and research in general.

In general, historians trace the origins of management education to the late 19th and early 20th centuries and to the countries such as France, Germany, United Kingdom, and the United States of America. These countries had developed a form of vocational education for practising managers in the areas of finance, accounting, management control and operations, and sales and distribution. A characteristic feature of this education was its inherently practical thrust and the overall objective was to enhance the skill sets of people working in business and industry. France had its *Ecoles de Commerce*, the United Kingdom had schools of commerce, and Germany called them, *Handelschochschulen*. Besides, there were the American business schools which played a key role in the consolidation and development of management education.

Following the establishment of Wharton Business School in 1881 and Harvard Business School in 1908, business schools grew faster in the United States thanks to private donations from the corporates and the philanthropists. Moreover, the United States had decisive say in laying down the future contours of management education, as they were the first to bring out management textbooks. For instance, Richard D. Irwin Publishing Company and the HBS Publishing took the lead in generating business texts and teaching material. Expectedly, the US business schools had control over curricula design and the accompanying learning resources. It is this historicity which gave the United States lead in establishing a certain benchmarking of what management education has been. And, it is the United States which has produced exemplars and leaders in the field of management education. Little wonder, the widely prevalent fact of the use of business school as a representative term testifies to the almost total US dominance over the field of management education.

In fact, it was in the United States where the first bachelor's programme in Business was introduced. Wharton's bachelor's program in business started in 1881 followed by Dartmouth's first master's degree in business in 1900 and Harvard's MBA degree in 1908. In other words, it was in the United States where concerted efforts to move management education to the world of academia and away from vocationalism, was made. Also, it was in the United States where the early setting up by a group of leading US business schools of the Association to Advance Collegiate Schools of Business (AACSB International) prompted an early attention to issues like scientific rigour, quality standards, certification and the like. Viewed thus, the continuing American leadership in management education, and its hitherto unchallenged status, has been an outcome of a range of factors with adequate historical depth: endowments and grants for the setting up of business schools, attention to curriculum, teaching resources and standardisation, and continual quest of academic legitimacy within the academy.

According to Thomas, Lorange, and Sheth (2013: 4), "the main purpose was to improve the relatively low societal and professional status of business managers, although impetus also came from military sources who pioneered the study of logistics, operations and operations research". Despite such efforts, one witnesses consistent and very strong resistance to the development and incorporation of management education as a formal academic discipline to be lodged in the higher portals of a university. It is this opposition which reflects the slow growth of management as a university discipline giving rise to serious legitimacy deficit and identity crisis. Its claims as a serious academic discipline have been severely contested. In fact, it has been viewed as a source of growing managerialism that undermines the fundamental ideals and visions of universities as creators of knowledge. For someone like Thorstein Veblen, an economist and sociologist in the early 20th century US, business education was incompatible with the collective cultural purpose of the university. He famously proclaimed 'a college of commerce belongs in the corporation of learning no more than a department of athletics' (cited in Thomas *et al* 2013: 68).

Many others too argued about its essentially remaining as some sort of training as part of the trade school era. The Nobel Laureate Herbert Simon provocatively termed it as 'wasteland of vocationalism'. Many others too thought of business education as typically catering for undergraduate students with some practicality-based master's programme. They would find much of it as descriptive and shorn of research inputs unlike other well-established academic disciplines. To be sure, given the original impetus of management education to impart specific vocational skills such as accounting and commerce with no liberal arts education in the curriculum, it continued to be seen as incompatible with the goals of the university, namely, both the pursuit of knowledge for its own sake and the application of knowledge to practical pursuits. It was this incompatibility that Herbert Simon had referred to and had exhorted business schools to follow them.

There was no open embrace of management education in the United Kingdom as well. In fact, because of the low academic esteem of management education, the prestigious universities like Cambridge and Oxford resisted the opening of business schools till 1990 and 1994, respectively. Indeed, there were schools of commerce in Birmingham (established in 1902) and Manchester (established in 1904). But they did not command much respect as their programme were not seen as much theory driven or theory oriented. In fact, business school came out of its low academic reputation only with the publication of Franks Report in 1963. This report did lift management education out of the shadow of its past much like what the earlier publication of reports that did the equivalent job in the United States like the Ford Foundation (Gordon and Howell 1959) and the Carnegie Foundation (Pierson 1959). For the first time in its history, these reports had the cumulative function of according the management education a respectability it sorely lacked, vied for but had barely managed for the first six to seven decades of its existence.

However, the Ford and Carnegie reports (both published in 1959) became the turning points in the recalibration and the reorientation of management education. Undoubtedly, they laid the foundations for much of what we see today that goes by the name of management. They have been the harbingers of injecting a research-oriented and discipline-based focus to management education, at least in the prestigious institutions in the field. Besides stressing analytical rigour, problem-solving ability, and scientific method, the Ford Report put a high premium on knowledge creation as the legitimate goal of management education much like any other established academic discipline. The Report also advocated the study of all business operations and functions from a broad integrated managerial perspective bringing in political, economic, and social environment, thereby facilitating legitimate entry of modern social sciences in management education. Likewise, the Carnegie Report brought in the quantitative aspects of scientific rigour including statistics, simulation, and operations research.

Indeed, these reports are the anchor-sheets for the subsequent growth and the prevailing structure of scholarly discipline-based academic research in management education. The recommendations of these reports helped business education overshadow its clinical and practical past, tuned to the relevance part of this long-continuing battle between relevance and rigour that we see even today. Once and for all, research became the defining feature of the field of management in all its expected nuances of academic rigour and protocols – methodological robustness, analytical acuity, and theoretical elegance. And, the academic publication on par with other established academic disciplines became the ultimate benchmark of scientific rigour that the much debated recommendations of Ford and Carnegie reports helped shape.

In the United Kingdom, Franks' policy recommendations led to the creation of London Business School and Manchester Business School as loosely integrated bodies with their parent universities in 1964. A little bit earlier, in the early 1960s, India too saw the setting up of standalone Indian Institutes of Management (IIMs) with the active support of the Ford Foundation. These IIMs were being set up in India in the early 1960s with the active collaboration of the US business school: the Sloan School of Management in the case of IIM Calcutta and the Harvard Business School (HBS) in the case of IIM Ahmedabad.

Even though much of the writings on management education remain steeped today in these unresolved tensions between the quest for scientific rigour (based on the philosophy and methodology of logical positivism) and the test of relevance (that is practical applied research directly feeding into management practices of the business firm), it is safe to say that the Ford and Carnegie reports sealed the destiny of management education towards the rigour end of the spectrum. In fact, the positivist academic model emanating out of these reports has been the dominant one since the 1960s. The model continues today despite periodic soul searching and vociferous complaints about the preponderance of arcane and esoteric academic research, poor training of the students, and the uncritical emulation of the models of physicists and economists rather than the more professional models of doctors and lawyers. There are occasional calls to turn management into a full-blown profession, a potential that has not been realised (Khurana and Nohria 2008). This envisaged professionalisation will strike a judicious balance between the analytical and action-oriented ends of management education while also ensuring a meticulous blend of the regional and the global thinking and orientation.

A cursory glance at the burgeoning literature (both academic and popular) around management education and profession is enough to convince us that much of the debate has been framed by the two conflicting and irreconcilable ideals of rigour and relevance. The ultimate blueprint of management education depends on the end of the spectrum one is wedded to. However, the debate can succinctly be understood in this framework with different people tilting towards different ends of the academic-professional (rigour-relevance) spectrum with the occasional throwing in of the rhetoric of ethical and visionary leadership, and the persistent clamour for synthesising the two in an ideal world of management theory and practice.

The American hegemony

Indeed, even today, the United States remains the ultimate arbiter of management education globally. As Starkey and Tiratsoo (2007: 122) rightly remark, 'because American schools have greater organisational coherence and bigger resource bases, they are able to monopolise judgements about what is good and what is not, and thus, in effect, simultaneously perpetuate their own superiority and force the rest of the world to follow them'. Publication in the American journals has become the norm. Degrees and credentials from the US business schools carry disproportionate weight in the job market. Research collaboration with colleagues based in the United States fetches academic dividends and ensures global academic recognition. Audit rankings and accreditation have their own corrosive effects on other knowledge traditions within the management field further cementing US domination of relevant definitions and meanings. Excellence in management education is invariably defined by whatever content the American wants to impute to the term. It is not that such form of academic dependence is exclusive to the field of management. However, whereas in many other fields of humanities and social sciences, this dependence has given rise to counter movements in the form of post-colonial theory, orientalism, and certain variants of post-structuralism, the field of management has so far seen only the emergence of the CMS as a reaction to the American hegemony and a counter movement to carve out alternative spaces of academic legitimacy and reputation.

Rather, the differences in the way management education have historically been organised are getting increasingly reduced though the centrality of the US model. For example, the understanding of capitalism has been more broad-based in Europe. The European discourse has usually been about transcending the prevalent buzzwords of shareholders' value and entrepreneurial capitalism. It has been more influenced by the social democratic forms of capitalism and has resultantly focussed more on the role of business in society and social responsibility of the business. Within Europe itself, there has been greater diversity and less institutional conformity in the context of management education. Germany and Scandinavian countries have been less receptive to management education. Likewise, management education has had late development in Eastern European countries, and that too under the US financial and advisory assistance. However, with the advent of the Bologna Accord in 1999, which sought to harmonise the framework of higher education degrees in EU countries, the trend towards convergence of institutional structures and curriculum design has gone apace. More than the legal imperative, it is the intense competition at internationalisation that is driving the drive towards uniformity of form and contents. Although accreditation bodies like AMBA and EQUIS in Europe claim to have differing philosophies of what management education is, in effect, they all cater to the American model. Most European countries consider it as a badge of honour to have a business school comparable to a US elite business school. With obvious differences in quality, the elite US business school models such as Chicago, Columbia, North-western, Stanford, and Wharton act as the reference models and there have been widespread attempts at emulation in the European countries as well. INSEAD in France is often projected like the US elite business school and so is London Business School.

Our argument is not that all business schools are alike or they follow a uniform standard syllabus for MBA. Instead, what we wish to highlight is the rapid institutional standardisation of management education. There is a definite movement towards homogeneity and mass production under the impetus of the American MBA as the worldly recognisable emblem of management education worldwide. Within this uniform aspirational structure, of course, there a rat race among the providers of management education to go for product differentiation to cater to the varying segments of the prospective market. This tendency can be noticed within the United States itself. For example, the HBS has historically distinguished itself by its case method pedagogy which its critics have found to be a rather stultifying best practice model not always leading to the development of analytical ability. The defenders of the case method have not only held the ground but the HBS has also been spearheading the movement globally to popularise the case method teaching to outwit, if not silence, its critics.

Contrary to Harvard Business School's anchoring in the case method, Chicago's Booth School of Business has been rooted in the culture of a discipline-based and strong social science research tradition exemplifying the best of scientific rigour. There is a new trend that is gaining ground in management education, that is, to offer more domain oriented MBAs like finance, technology to capitalise on their strengths of geographical proximity to a finance district or a technology hub. London Business School is frequently cited as a model to have allied its offerings to the domain of finance to optimise on its proximity to London Financial District. Likewise, the business school at the University of California, San Diego, is credited with institutional innovation in the field of an alignment of the technology and management fields to leverage its locational advantage in a technology 'hot spot'.

Understandably, a business school's culture tends to be shaped by historical roots anchored to a discipline or pedagogy. For example, the University of Chicago, the Wharton School and the University of Rochester are anchored to finance and economics. Yale and Stanford focus more on global perspectives including culture, history, political and economic issues. Most European business schools are anchored to theory in economic and social sciences. In the United Kingdom, their foci have also included CMS and an emphasis on both humanities and public management (Thomas *et al* 2013: 151).

The Lancaster and Warwick business schools emphasise strong social science-based research. There are differences coming out of the historicity of national contexts. In general, the UK business schools show more openness to social sciences. Moreover, in the United Kingdom, there is another type of reaction against the prevalence of analytic positivist research – the rise of the Critical Management Studies (to be discussed in Chapter 4). While UK business schools emphasise the academic side of the academic-professional spectrum, their ideological critique of capitalism has made them the champion of CMS (Fournier and Grey 2000). As a consequence, some of them employ a research-based, evidence-based social science framework emphasising multidisciplinary traditions. They put a high premium on increased historical understanding of cultural and global contexts. They advocate the kind of critical analytical thinking which would address such questions as under what enabling conditions markets work well and when they do not. They consider management problems to be messier and ambiguous underlining the need for an interdisciplinary approach. For that reason, they critique the earlier type of discipline-based reductionist analytical models informed by logical positivism. They raise wider questions relating to personal private gains versus serving societal needs.

For some of them, business schools are no more than a finishing school for senior management. For others too, they act as necessary rite of institutional passage facilitating anticipatory socialisation in the business world. They question the very purpose of the business school and ask if it could ever act as intellectual liberal cauldron for the pursuit of disinterested knowledge. They find business schools to be increasingly dictated by industry rather than the pursuit of scholarship. They also hold business schools as the catalyst and stimulus for the increasing commercialisation of higher education. They would like to assess business schools in terms of their contributions to society. They expect business schools to extend and amplify the ethical and moral compass of the hitherto narrowly defined management education by bringing in issues such as health, poverty, sustainability, natural disasters, corporate social responsibility, and the problems of globalisation and urbanisation. For them, the sole preoccupation with imparting problem-solving and decision-making skills to a narrow band of business elites should not be seen as the ultimate purpose of a business school (Grey 2007).

There still remains a lingering critique of the field of management. Critics of the field often point out as to how management scholars have marginal presence as public intellectuals even in the United States. Almost everywhere, they have little impact on public policy debates. For them, there still is considerable academic uncertainty leading to status anxieties on the part of management scholars. They remain quite unsure about their academic standing amidst doubts and hesitancy on the part of their peers to accord them legitimate academic peerage. Not surprisingly, the Ford Foundation report characterised the field as 'an uncertain giant, gnawed by doubt and harassed by the barbs of unfriendly critics' (Pierson 1959: 4). Even today, critics charge management education as being anchored in a narrow frame of reference despite allusions to cultural differences, fairness, and social responsibility, and sustainability. They ridicule the consistent invocation of critical thinking as a buzzword on the part of management academics at a time when the field is moving away from its historical association with critical social sciences. We keep hearing *ad nauseum* that those enrolling for the MBA have limited though clearly thought out ambitions. They know what they want. And, what they want, above all, is a quick and uncomplicated grounding in those skills that will advantage them on graduation in the corporate job market. What they do not want, by contrast, is anything that departs from this agenda.

In this context, management curriculum turns out to be simply reflective of the market demand. Not only is critical thinking simply absent from much of market-driven curriculum, but is also seen rather a deviation and a frill to be judged harshly by the career-centric student-customers. The overwhelming desire is for teaching that is straightforward and uncomplicated. The majority of students do not want any ifs and buts or the questioning ambiguity. What they want is straightforward grabbing of the marketable credentials (Thomas et al 2013: 105). Some people do think of MBAs as grasping and intellectually shallow, uniquely superficial or blinkered. They never tire of invoking Harold Leavitt's evocative characterisation of MBAs as 'critters with lop-sided brains, icy hearts, and shrunken souls' (39). For the partisans to this thinking, MBA, though lucrative, is essentially a degree that lacks real intellectual merit and hardly reveals any depth of scholarship. MBA is more about gimmicks and fashions, media management, rankings, recruitment, and placement. Accreditation and rankings remain institutional obsessions of the business schools. These people characterise business schools as academic treadmills solely concerned with the volume of output regardless of almost any other consideration. For them, expediency, as a rule, overrides scholarly values.

Conclusion

For the larger part of its existence, management education has been caught up with the choice between Scylla of the academic model and the Charybdis of the professional model (Starkey and Tiratsoo 2007: 211). Much of the contemporary debate, too, is about the exercise of the same choice which really boils down to two basic approaches – getting closer to real world of managers or getting closer to the academy (Starkey and Tiratsoo 2007: 205). It is also true that for much of the twentieth century, at least during the first six decades, management and business research was too practical to go for serious academic reckoning by the university establishment notwithstanding Taylor's clarion call of scientific management. Sure enough, it has had an arguably narrow scholarly compass as well as limited scope of application. Also, it was small-scale in operation and over-functional in its conceptualisation. Rarely did it feel the need to collaborate with the other disciplines dealing with the larger affairs of man and society, and rarely did it get enriched by the insights of other disciplines. As a consequence, business and management research was long considered to be a poor relation of many more established academic disciplines. The larger university community was distinctly unenthusiastic about the quality of management research. In their assessment, management research had to travel some way before it could be considered genuinely first class in any meaningfully comparative sense (Starkey and Tiratsoo 2007: 120).

However, in recent times, the tide has turned in favour of management in all possible senses of term, and it has acquired a distinctive individuality of its own owing to factors such as its increased institutional visibility, its enhanced attraction as a professional programme, its rising academic legitimacy, its growing research stature and its ever-developing capacity to offer prestigious and gainful employment to the ever-growing numbers of academics belonging to a range of related disciplines. In terms of research, too, its reliance on related disciplines has gone down even though it does not have a paradigm development of its own. In any case, it no longer looks like a melting pot of disciplinary perspectives of the yore. Yet, the related disciplines have not become totally irrelevant to its growth and development. As Agrawal and Hoetkar (2007) find out, its sequential reliance on psychology overshadows its reliance on economics and sociology in terms of micro research, though some reliance on economics and sociology in terms of macro-research continues apace.

So far as the overall connect with the other areas of social sciences is concerned, it is surely on the decline. Given the prevailing incentive structure in business schools and the proliferation of management journals (and their rank orderings for the purpose of accreditation), management academics are institutionally encouraged to publish less in the journals of related disciplines and more in their 'own' ones. This reveals a new compact animating the overarching urge to mark its existence as a stand-alone and respectable disciplinary field, albeit with historical support from social and decision sciences. Occasionally, one does come across feeble voices reiterating the wider compact between business schools and business and society with the attendant imperative to draw on the full range of social sciences along with arts and humanities (Grey 2007; Starkey and Tiratsoo 2007). Arguably, there is resonant critique of the fundamental paradigm that informs management as a disciplinary field – a curious mix of unrestrained pursuit of self-interest, market fundamentalism, and minimal state intervention. But this paradigm has been lodged so firmly for so long that it is difficult to jettison it straightaway for it privileges certain types of knowledge, and thereby, certain types of possessors of that knowledge the academic elites.

When it comes to sociology, it is important to remember that it is largely seen as an import from somewhere else. Sociologists, too, do not quite find themselves 'at home' in this new academic-intellectual terrain. After all, management itself is such a new academic habitat that almost everything is likely to appear as exogenous to the field. Its intellectual and institutional novelty apart, over the past six decades, it has successfully acquired the substance and veneer of a modern academic formation with all the attendant paraphernalia of journals, conferences, professional associations, texts and readers, degrees and diplomas, and the like. No wonder, it attracts many migrants from other conventional subject areas like economics, mathematics, psychology, sociology, etc., who may not feel quite at home there but who may find themselves too ensconced in their new setting to contemplate any immediate or long-term departure. As of now, the new habitat is utterly attractive, and the older institutional homes of conventional social sciences (probably save economics) are on steady decline. So, for a discipline like sociology the choices are limited. It has to keep arguing its case for relevance to management education and research either in terms of its past contributions to the field of industrial relations (the classic invocation of Elton Mayo) or in terms of its real and potential academic yield in the field of sociology of work, employment and organisations (the glorious invocation of Max Weber figuring as a pioneering theorist for the study of that most rational of rational-legal organisation – the bureaucracy).

So the question is not to speculate if sociology has been indigenous to the business school or an inalienable part of management education historically. Instead, the real task is map out sociological practices in relation to the institutional setting of a management institute. In the next chapter, we undertake this task by examining the place of sociology primarily in institutions of management. This exercise reveals both the way management education has unfolded itself in India in relation to cognate disciplines like sociology and the way sociology has been able to contribute (or not contribute) to the field of management owing to the particularities of its national trajectory. The next chapter has as in-built comparative focus for the purpose of highlighting the national-geographical variability of the emergence of new academic disciplines and their contingent public acceptance and institutional legitimacy.

Notes

1. Sociology's profile as a policy-relevant discipline in the United States was enhanced when the President Herbert Hoover appointed two sociologists (William Ogburn and Howard Odum), on *the President's Committee on Social Trends*. Established in 1929, the Committee comprised a group of leading social scientists whose task was to collect data on leading social institutions and behaviour. The chairman of the committee was Wesley Mitchell, Columbia University economist and director of the National Bureau for Economic Research. The committee's vice-chairman was Charles Merriam, founder of the Social Science Research Council (SSRC). The Committee's final product, *Recent Social Trends*, was published in early 1932 with over 1,500 pages (Bannister 1987).

2. Elton Mayo (1880–1949) was one of the key figures involved in Hawthorne Studies and his work laid the foundation for the many later management and organisational thinking. He worked in areas of motivation and commitment, and worker-management relations and came to occupy a legendary status as a pioneer of applied social science, especially in the workplace. He emphasised that work is a group activity, that it is social, and that the peer group (informal groups) is highly significant in work relationships. According to him, workers are influenced by social demands inside and outside work, alongside formal structures and groups. His plea was to harness informal groups for greater productivity. He is generally credited with the use of sociological theories in the field of industrial relations (see Smith 1998: 221–249).

3 Meandering pathways
Betwixt the national and the global

Management education: the Indian context

This chapter examines the interactions between sociology and management education in India. Drawing upon the disciplinary history of Indian sociology, it brings out the limited nature of interactions between the two disciplines in the context of the overwhelming institutional sway of the university system. The university-dominated structure and focus of Indian sociology has somehow made sociologists in India ill-equipped to work in applied interdisciplinary settings. Besides mapping out sociological practices in relation to management education and research, the chapter assesses the contributions of sociology to the consolidation and transformation of management studies as an academic field. This chapter particularly focuses on the competing demands of national distinctiveness and global excellence that institutions of management education in India have been subjected to. The chapter also hints at the limitations of a homogenising vision of management education that is being promoted in the name of global benchmarking.

Management education has witnessed a spectacular growth in India in the past half a century. In a way, it appears to have occupied the pride of place in professional higher education. With every passing year, the number of both those aspiring to get admission in a management institute/department, and those succeeding in securing one, is on the upswing. A management degree has come to be seen as the proverbial icing on the cake. Not surprisingly, a large number of engineering graduates, including the ones from Indian Institutes of Technology (IITs), National Institutes of Technology (NITs), and other prestigious engineering colleges, routinely go for a management degree, or at least seriously try to have one. This trend has imparted management education with a glamour that is generally absent from other programmes

DOI: 10.4324/9781003257813-3

of education. Sure enough, India's burgeoning economy, fuelled by a growing middle class, has made the MBA a more valuable degree than ever before.

As Starkey and Tiratsoo (2007: 117) rightly remark that this was not always the case. In fact, after Independence, the old objective of producing *babu* and later civil servants gave way to joining the engineering stream at one of the reputed IITs. In the initial decades after Independence, the MBA was not the most glamorous degree. Subsequently, it started getting seen as an additional credential after the mandatorily attractive B. Tech degree. At present, it has become a *sine qua non* for aspiring young people given to upward career mobility and the globally mobile lucrative assignments even as the most preferred route into management education continues to pass through the engineering degree. The attractiveness of a management degree has grown so much in stature that now an engineering degree looks like a mere prelude to the ultimate MBA degree. In itself and by itself, an engineering degree looks totally inadequate. Such changes cannot be understood merely in terms of the internal dynamics of the system of higher education and the attendant shifts in the prestige hierarchy of disciplines within it.

There have been larger external forces at work. At least two of them can be singled out for consideration in terms of their implications for prestigious white-collar jobs in the country. First, the economic reforms of 1991 opened up a new vista of employment opportunities in the corporate sector including multinational corporations. The opening up of the economy brought into the realm of possible jobs in such fields as consulting, investment banking, and fintech for which an MBA degree was the most potent resource. Second, the implementation of reservations in public employment for the Other Backward Classes (OBCs) rendered government jobs more competitive. Coincidentally, the second happened around the same time as the first. Evidently, the established middle classes gravitated towards management degrees which would facilitate their access to private corporate sector where there is no reservation. These national developments coincided with the global success of capitalism as an unchallenged ideology which emerged triumphant after the collapse of the then Union of Soviet Socialist Republics (USSR). Capitalism started penetrating new geographies and culture areas including countries like China which had the formal veneer of a socialist economy. The former socialist bloc countries of Eastern Europe too started embracing capitalism with a newfound gusto. In a way, this globally victorious march of capitalism as an inevitable ideology of organising economic activities and its widespread acceptance did play a role in preparing the congenial ideological ground for an easy acceptance of management education which has had its long and intimate association with shareholder's capitalism.

Against this backdrop, it would be unfair to say that management education is just a shortcut to the upward career mobility, or the much-touted ticket, to enter the lucrative high-end corporate job market. This premature dismissal would amount to overlooking the dynamics that inform the changing fortunes of an academic discipline, and the host of factors that shape those dynamics (see Chapter 1). Likewise, it would be hasty to dismiss it simply as a manifestation of the extant global trend in higher education for management education in India presents several distinguishing features of its own. Noticeably, management education does not share with other established academic disciplines of sciences, social science, and engineering its origins as part of India's encounter with colonial modernity. It made its benevolent entry onto the Indian scene without any colonial baggage after India had attained its Independence in 1947. It could very well be projected as a benign import from the oldest democracy to the largest one along with other types of intellectual/institutional support in the fields of community development, agricultural extension activities (including some of the agricultural universities in India modelled after the land-grant universities of the United States), the area studies and the like. Moreover, this entry was mediated by large philanthropic foundations (for example, the Ford Foundation). It was not a straightforward official bilateral co-operation between two states that one had witnessed in the setting up of some of the older IITs.

Secondly, the introduction of management in India coincided with the heyday of centrally controlled planned economy. And, no one noticed much contradiction between the context and the new import. Thus, Professor S. Nurul Hasan, the then Minister of Education, had reminded the graduating students of the heavy public investment in their education and exhorted them to contribute to society at large. His remarks on the occasion of the 7th Convocation of IIM Calcutta (on 15 April 1972) underlined 'a wider vision, a sense of social awareness, and social responsibility, an identification with the masses of the people, a deep sympathy for their travails and sufferings, and a passionate commitment to improving their condition in the shortest possible time'. According to him, the managers must learn to 'subordinate corporate profits, or personal gains, to the development of the economy as a whole, to the promotion of self-reliance in the country, and to the welfare of the suffering millions'. Interestingly, Hasan urged the graduating students to dedicate themselves *to the cause of achievement of Socialism in our country* and to utilise 'their knowledge, expertise and skills, for building up a better world for the common man of India' (emphasis mine; IIMC 1987: 46–7).

In fact, by the late 1950s, six Indian universities had already introduced business management in their curriculum under the impetus of the All India Council of Technical Education (AICTE) and All India Management Association (AIMA); it was already functional in the field of management training and development (Chatterjee 1982; Sheth 1991). Interestingly, the underlying philosophy of management education, that is, to further the interests of shareholders' value of a capitalist firm, was played down in the Indian context. Instead, management education was portrayed as crucial for enhancing the efficiency of the public sector units (PSUs) that were to be the commanding heights of the Indian economy during the Nehruvian era. It was fervently believed that public servants having some kind of training in management would help in the optimal allocation and efficient utilisation of scarce resources that the country had. That is why the initial clientele for management education was to be people already working in the public and private sectors than the fresh young men and women aspiring for an attractive career.

Interestingly enough, in an intellectual climate characterised by the calls for 'decolonisation of Indian mind' and the quest for indigenous knowledge traditions and theories (in the wake of national optimism brought in by Indian Independence), one does not find any serious opposition to the import of management education in the country. Indeed, in the 1950s, some Indian academics had raised issues about American neo-imperialism in the context of the consistent influx of Area Studies scholars to India for the study of Indian society and culture. However, this concern did not include the newly introduced field of management. It would be safe to assert that, given its novelty and its lack of colonial baggage, management education has had a smooth institutional and political sailing in India. In due course though, its heavy reliance on American models and materials would come in for heavy criticism. Calls for indigenisation would frequently be made, and some of the scholars in their intellectual zeal would turn to Indian scriptures for management insights and demonstrate that these ancient scriptures, anyway, have been the great repositories of the theories and practices of modern management (Chakraborty 1997; Chatterjee 2012).

It is not that everyone was convinced of the alien character of the management education. Some argued to the contrary. For instance, Ravi Matthai, an eminent institution-builder, asserts, 'The character of management education that has evolved [in India] is not a foreign transplant, nor is it merely a foreign adaptation, but represents creation of Indian mind, dedicated to working on the problems of their own country' (Matthai 1980: M69). He is insistent on acknowledging a distinctive indigenous character of management education in India. According to him, in India management education has not been concerned with the industry alone but with the wider economic and social problems of the country. This contrasts sharply with the United States, where the pre-eminent focus of management education has been on industry. To substantiate his assertion, he underlines the initiatives of the two of the most prestigious IIMs: that the IIMA worked for the application of management ideas to sectors of primary national significance, that is, agriculture, and the IIMC worked in the area of population control.

In any case, there is no denying the simple point that management education started its journey in India on almost a clean slate without having been embroiled in the debate encompassing colonial forms of knowledge. It almost has had an open embrace by an expanding system of higher education in a post-colonial country. In no time, management education got firmly lodged at the very centre of the Indian academic establishment. Some of the institutions imparting management education started getting global recognition as well. The elite management institutions now operate in the global arena by virtue of their participation in international accreditation and other types of rankings conducted by various agencies. Since the 1990s, the new trend has gathered momentum wherein the new generation of professionals are no longer trained in liberal arts colleges and conventional multi-disciplinary universities but in stand-alone institutions of management and technology. This has led to the increase in number of such institutions: India today boasts of 23 IITs and 20 IIMs. And evidently, their public prestige has been on the upswing as compared to the state-funded universities. However, it needs to be borne in mind that most of the universities too impart management education through their faculties/departments of management.

So far as the premier institutions of management education like IIMs are concerned, they were consciously sought to be modelled after the American business schools. George W. Robbins, the then Associate Dean of the School of Business Administration, University of California, Los Angeles, was the consultant hired by the Planning Commission, who put forward the blueprint for an all-India Institute of Management (Planning Commission 1957; Robbins 1959). Accordingly, with the active institutional collaboration of Alfred P. Sloan School of

Management, MIT, the first IIM was established in Calcutta in 1961. Likewise, the IIM Ahmedabad was established in 1962 with the active institutional support of the Harvard Business School. Given the overall national drive towards industrialisation, IIMs were created with the apparent objectives of (a) meeting the needs of Industry, Commerce, and Government for managerial manpower, (b) assisting in the solution of management problems, and (c) developing an indigenous literature on management through an effective programme of teaching, research, consultation, and publication. It was generally believed that capital and technology alone did not lead to growth unless sound management acted as a catalyst. Expectedly, management was seen as the missing element in the would-be gigantic industrial enterprise unfolding before the nation – a gap that would be filled by the newly created institutions of management (Thakur 2010).

Many thought management education to be a creative endeavour in the sense of being an essential element in the process of modernisation and in the building of a new social and economic order. Given the spirit of the time, the enthronement of professional manager as the chief director of economic activity in the country was seen as a much-awaited progressive development. Some of them were ecstatic in viewing managers as great change agents capable of overcoming our backwardness and 'to change our traditional, underdeveloped society into a modern industrialised one' (IIMC 1987: 34). For example, Bhaskar Mitter, the then chairman of Andrew Yule & Co., appears to be at his rhetorical best at the 6th convocation ceremony at IIM Calcutta (on 12 April 1971). Mitter was jubilant to note that many of the best brains in the country were choosing management as a career, just as at one time the intellectual elite of the country tended to converge towards the ICS. For him, the managers are the ultimate development warriors ever-willing to fight *'on the shop-floors and in the fields, at the desks, drawing boards and in the market place'*. In his understanding, the manager *'who can organise the campaigns for these battles and win them successfully is making more useful contribution towards the transformation of his country than the abstract theorist'* (emphasis mine, IIMC 1987: 40).

Apparently, the then policymakers did not see any conflict of interests between the propagation of management education through the establishment of IIMs, and the pursuit of socialistic pattern of society as a consensual national goal. Rather, IIMs were expected to professionally contribute to the grand ideal of building a socialistic society where public sectors would occupy the commanding heights. Management training was seen as crucial for the efficient and profitable management of public sector enterprises so that persons from administrative services were gradually replaced by the newly trained managers to cut down delays in decisions and thereby enhance profits and productivity and contribute to the socialist pattern of society. D. R. Gadgil, the then Deputy Chairman of the Planning Commission, remarked that the cadre of business executives and managers to be built with the help of IIMs would help make the much-needed transition from 'enterprises managed largely on the model of the administrative department to enterprises managed essentially as autonomous business units' (IIMC 1987: 17).

There was another implicit ideal animating the growing enterprise of management education, that of facilitating and reinforcing the processes of nascent industrial democratisation in the country. Delivering the first convocation address (on 16 May 1966), Shri Sachin Chaudhury, the then Finance Minister of India, lauded the attempt to bring in industrial management on the basis of professional competence for its potential to offset the strong allegiance to family and caste characterising business communities in India. According to him, professional management would limit the undesirable concentration of control over many firms in a few hands with undesirable social consequences. He sees inevitable connection between the emergence of industrial managers as a professional group and the vision of a democratic society in the second half of the 20th century. Expectedly, he conceives of managerial responsibilities in a much wider way – well beyond the shareholders alone, or the task of ensuring a good rate of return on capital invested, or the expansion of the firms concerned. A manager's responsibility has to be 'towards labour, towards others who work with you, and more important of all towards society' (*Ibid.*: 5). He added, 'A good manager has also to look beyond the wealth and welfare of any particular firm he manages. *It should be the philosophy of top management that the interests of its business shall not run counter to public good, but will promote it*' (*Ibid.*: 6).

Additionally, the newly minted managers were expected to ensure that the development of the private sector was in keeping with the interest of the community at large: 'it is of the utmost importance that the management of private industry and business should also be entrusted increasingly to professional managers rather than to persons whose right to management is based on ownership of personal wealth or the accident of birth' (IIMC 1987: 4). In essence, the higher ideal of an industrial democracy appears to have animated the vision in the sense of the envisaged separation of purely managerial functions from ownership of capital or wealth. More importantly, the private sector was expected to add to the processes of industrial democratisation by entrusting its management increasingly to professional people. Viewed thus, management education was seen as contributing to public good by virtue of its revolutionary potential to transform the managerial practices of the private sector as well, which were considered to be regressively anchored in the networks of family, kinship, caste, and community. Sure enough, management education was the much-admired and the much-valued public good with immense benefits to national goals of democracy and development.

Against this backdrop of evolving changing vision of management education in India over the past half a century, in this chapter, we attempt to map out the transforming configurations of academic interactions between management and the related disciplines with a particular focus on sociology. We try to enlist the factors shaping such interactions. As part of this endeavour, we look at the disciplinary history of sociology in India to argue its growing distance from management. Our framework integrates the changes in the fields of both management and sociology to present a historical and contemporary outline of their intersectionality and what we claim to be its diminishing scope as management education took off on its own steam. In particular, we spotlight such aspects of disciplinary history of sociology in India which arguably led to its growing unattractiveness, if not total incompatibility, for the expanding landscape of management education in the country.

A caveat is in order, though. In the case of India, we are essentially dealing with a minuscule scale of interaction between sociology and management education. Unlike the United States and the United Kingdom, a handful of sociologists are part of the institutions of management in India, and their numbers are increasingly declining. Put differently, sociologists are numerically too insignificant in institutions of management education in India to carry any academic weight. In the beginning, when management education was taking institutional shape, it did pull in academics from related academic disciplines like economics, sociology, anthropology, and psychology. However, as the IIMs and other institutions started producing their own doctorates, whatever limited traffic that management institutes have had with the universities and other related disciplines has almost come to a naught. Also, over the years, the internal specialisms in management themselves have got institutionalised. Now, the system has enough internally trained professionals that obviate the need for any continued dependence on related disciplines like sociology. If there is an academic with professional credentials in Human

Resources Management (HRM) or Organisational Behaviour (OB) or marketing, obviously, there is no need to look for a sociologist with research experience in the field of work and employment or in organisation studies or in other relevant fields. Areas of management like strategy, business policy, and international business have developed their own academic niche and no longer seem to need the services of trained people from related 'mother' disciplines.

Sociology in management education in India

Gone are the days when there was palpable institutional and scholarly hesitation about the appropriateness of management as a taught programme of education or a distinctive academic discipline. As we have seen in Chapter 2, for quite some time, management was considered to be some kind of academic *potpourri* drawing parasitically on the established social sciences and other academic disciplines. The chequered trajectory of its origins, evolution, and the subsequent transformation as an attractive discipline has not only established management education in India but has also accorded it a relatively higher status in the disciplinary hierarchy of the academy. It is certainly valued much more favourably when compared to other social sciences, sociology in particular. This newfound confidence in management as a discipline of the contemporary constitutes the backdrop against which the place of sociology is being discussed in what follows, including the politics of disciplinary hierarchy (Thakur 2017).

The plain fact is that sociology has marginal, if not altogether invisible, presence in management education in the country. Sociologists' negligible numbers in institutions of management apart, sociology in India has not been able to demonstrate its usefulness and relevance to the field of management education. This is largely because of the peculiarities of its disciplinary history to which we devote considerable attention in this chapter. Also, there has been an increasingly constrictive vision of management education that has taken hold of the new generation of educators and institution-builders. Sociology in India is seen much more distant from management when compared to other countries. A sociologist does not feel quite at home in an institution of management where the overwhelming discourse privileges the supposedly functional areas of management like finance and marketing.

In other countries, sociologists have been able to enter some of the areas of management like strategy, organisational behaviour, human resources management, marketing by virtue of their research contributions in the relevant fields. In India, this has hardly happened due to the sheer lack of relevant research in these fields. Expectedly, the onus is on sociologists to demonstrate that his/her work in sociology is relevant to management. In the early days of management education, sociologists could somehow sell their well-intentioned but suspect claims of their expertise in areas such as labour problems, trade unions, industrial sociology, and entrepreneurship. Those were also the days of a certain openness on the part of academic leaders who would welcome a sociologist amidst them for her sheer disciplinary expertise to impart a critical contextual perspective on business and society irrespective of immediate usefulness of her specialisation to management. Seen thus, sociology's presence in management in India does not seem to have a well-thought-out script. It has been muddled in a way, dependent more on the contingent presence of a handful of sociologists by accident. This has had enormous implications for its contributions to the field of management education and its public image as a related discipline of management.

When one looks at the place of sociology in management education in its entirety, that is, teaching, research, training, and consultancy, the emergent narrative is that of marginalisation (self-perceived or otherwise). As indicated earlier, the numbers matter, and sociologists are few and far between in institutions of management. But the marginal location of the sociologists is not a function of numbers alone. As we argue in what follows, it has much more to do with their disciplinary practices. Indeed, it is true that doing sociology in India is not a very respectable academic endeavour. So, naturally, that sense of disciplinary marginalisation will rub in irrespective of their institutional location. However, a sociology course in an institution of management is, by definition, less valuable compared to the courses in functional areas of management. More often than not, it is seen as an add-on than a real value addition. For a management student, sociology courses are unnecessary deviations from their primary tasks of self-fashioning as future managers. The playing institutional field itself is not levelled enough wherein other courses acquire weight and glamour beforehand. It leads to an expected, but peculiar, institutional hierarchy of the mainstream and the margins. And, the margins may feel patronised even in the best of times. To put it bluntly, social sciences in general occupy a marginal location within these institutions of management howsoever lofty the original ideals might have been to have them along with the core disciplines of management in the first place. The pertinent question is whether the marginalisation of social sciences in general, and sociology in particular, is inherent to the design and philosophy of management education.

As we have discussed in Chapter 2, that does not appear to be the case. On the contrary, we have argued that a combination of external and internal factors leads to the changing fortunes of any academic discipline. Going by that framework, it would be foolhardy to put all the blame on the institutions of management alone. The larger share of the blame needs to be apportioned by the disciplinary mainstream of sociology in India, which too accorded an indifferent reception to sociologists working in non-university settings. For a sociologist in India, working in a setting other than a multi-disciplinary university does not facilitate an easy professional approbation. In the setting of a university, a sociologist has the advantage of basking in the glory of the accumulated prestige and the acquired glamour of the institution/ she is working at. The disciplinary legacy factors effortlessly rub on the individual professional trajectory of a sociologist in a university. For the sociologist working in an institution of management, she has to acquire that professional prestige by her own unaided efforts, and that too, in not a very congenial institutional surroundings.

Admittedly, despite the downgrading of social sciences and liberal disciplines in general in the context of the withdrawal of the state from the public funding of universities and the increasing competition from the emerging market-friendly disciplines such as management, commerce, information technology, data analytics, and the like, sociological research and teaching appear to be firmly anchored in the universities and social science research institutions than in the institutions of management This can be seen in terms of publications issuing from prestigious publishing houses, the composition of membership of curriculum development committees of the University Grants Commission (UGC) and the Subject Advisory Committee of the Indian Council of Social Science Research (ICSSR), the sources of change in research interests and disciplinary foci, and the overall professional leadership which generally come from universities.

Of course, this proposition does not apply across the board but only to the few elite universities. Deshpande (2001: 9) puts it aptly, 'most of the time, most of those who refer to "Indian Sociology" are usually only referring to whatever is happening in/from a small number of elite institutions. Greatly (some may say overwhelmingly) dominated by the city of Delhi and its two major universities, this elite set of institutions also includes such well-known "regional" centres as Chandigarh, Hyderabad, Mumbai or Pune'. Otherwise, a careful observer of the institutional landscape of Indian sociology and its regional divisions and hierarchies, it is instructive to note that even Deshpande's meticulous mapping of the practices of discipline has no reference to professional institutions where sociology has some presence, be it the institutions of management, technology, medical and nursing colleges, and agricultural universities. True, universities nourish and sustain disciplinary traditions through their teaching programmes and research degrees. A university, despite all its limitations, creates future torchbearers of the disciplinary culture by virtue of its focus on post-graduate teaching and subsequent research, thus imparting continuity to the traditions of disciplinary learning. A professional institution other than a university does not have to carry the burden of this mandate. But then, a university sociologist does not have to carry (and hardly carries) the same burden of relevance that a sociologist based in a non-university setting has to carry (at least theoretically). As a consequence, the existential dilemmas for sociologists working in universities and other professional institutions are of a different order altogether (for a consideration of issues of relevance and the attendant policy-research interface in the Indian context see Thakur 2006). Besides, the idea of relevance comes to acquire a distinctive applied orientation, and a sociologist working in a professional institution has to naturally gravitate towards those issues/themes that have 'relevance' in her immediate institutional context.

The marginal place of sociology in institutions of management is not the function of the academic calibre of sociologists alone. Nor is it merely a function of their abysmally low numbers. It also emanates from, as we have seen in Chapter 2, the supposed lack of scientificity of sociology as an academic discipline. Sociologists very often have to travel the extra mile to convince themselves as well as those around them that sociology is an empirical and scientific discipline, just a few rungs below the natural sciences. This public image of sociology as a 'soft' and a less scientific discipline is the most fundamental source of the inferiority complex marking sociologists working in institutions of management.

This sense is acute in the field of professional education as the latter is seen as the natural habitat of hard, quantitative, and scientific disciplines. The institutional specificities of an institution of management thereby condemn sociologists to be in the company of disciplinary superiors. This contrasts with the institutional context of a multi-disciplinary university where there are a host of other 'soft' disciplines legitimately co-existing with the full-blown sciences. This is not to argue that a university is free from the evaluative implications of the hierarchy of academic disciplines. But, a university, or the idea of a university as it has been historically conceived, allows for the legitimate claims of all kinds of academic disciplines, including the humanities (Collini 2012, 2018). As Machlup (1994) argues, something is inferior to something else in relation to a particular quality provided that quality is highly valued and whose absence is seriously missed regardless of other qualities present. Moving further, one can think of different possibilities: (a) inferiority might make things desirable (e.g. sandpaper because of its inferior smoothness, anthropology because of its ability to generate meaningful insights in a micro-setting), (b) inferiority may be simply a matter of indifference (c) inferiority may be simply regrettable, nonetheless wanted, (e.g. psychiatry is required without its ability to effect quick cures, biology is essential without the lack of internal consistency in its theoretical systems).

Wherever something is inferior-superior with respect to the same attribute, there is a choice to be made between alternatives. That would mean in the context of natural and social sciences (a) banishment, (b) no allocation of resources, (c) discouraging the gifted from social sciences and pushing them for 'superior' pursuits, and (d) withholding respect from social scientists. However, these possibilities are out of question as natural sciences and social sciences cannot be, by any means, regarded as alternatives. Both are needed, and neither can be dispensed with. A pragmatic approach demands that something is done to improve social sciences like sociology and remedy their 'defects' or 'inadequacies' to bring them on par with other respectable scientific disciplines in an institution of management. But from the perspective of philosophy of science, these defects are differences and not *defects per se*.

That there are more variety and changes in social phenomena because of the large number of relevant variables and the impossibility of controlled experiment, that hypothesis in social sciences cannot be verified, that no numerical constants can be detected in the social world are not defects but fundamental principles to be grasped, accepted and taken into account. Indisputably, all differences need not lead to hierarchy, and inferiority is context bound. Very often, management educators fail to appreciate this plain proposition that because of these properties, research and analyses in social sciences hold greater complexity and difficulties, and possibly greater challenges (*Ibid.*: 5–19). They should not be dismissed as unscientific simply because they do not lend themselves to numerical value and cannot be analysed statistically. Problems presented by the social world are certainly not unimportant, and if they are also difficult to tackle, they ought to attract ample resources and the best minds. Unfortunately, neither is forthcoming in India as elsewhere.

Seen thus, the inferiority of sociology in the context of management education boils down to the place social sciences are accorded by the society and the political priorities of resource allocation, both human and financial, by the state. In other words, the place of sociology in institutions of management cannot be understood in relation to the latter's internal politics of knowledge. The place within is inextricably linked to the place without. And, sure enough, the latter is conditioned by a range of extraneous factors outlined in Chapter 1. In the ultimate analysis, an academic discipline's status is equally reflective of the political priorities of the state and the reigning sense of relevance and impact. The politics of knowledge production within the academy dynamically interact with these priorities and get translated into the variable availability and allocation of resources across institutions and disciplines. The point is that the marginalisation of an academic discipline like sociology (or social sciences in general) is not only institutionally ordained but also politically orchestrated.

In any case, sociology has too perfunctory a presence in management curriculum to merit a detailed discussion. Generally speaking, an MBA consists of two sets of courses the compulsory (core) package and the elective (optional) package. Largely, the compulsory courses are offered in the first year and the elective ones in the second year. The stated aim of the compulsory courses is to provide the students with the fundamental knowledge, skills and techniques, contextual understanding, and overall perspective necessary for general management. Compulsory courses are intended to offer broad training to students that will be useful to them in terms of career flexibility and mobility. At least, such courses attempt to equip students with requisite skills that facilitate their move towards general management positions. On the other hand, elective courses have the ostensible purpose of helping students develop an in-depth understanding of areas of their interest. Through such courses, students may choose to concentrate on particular topics or areas of their interest, if they wish. Since most of them are likely to start their careers in one of the functional areas, the specialization through elective courses is geared towards building the special skills required for those areas. Some typical electives courses generally crowd around areas of marketing, finance, strategy and international business, and human resources management.

It is to be noted that the curriculum is also an important ingredient of accreditation and other types of ranking of management institutions undertaken by the popular media. Arguably, there is intense pressure on these institutions to package their curriculum as updated and global (whatever that means). A cutting-edge curriculum is an

Meandering pathways 55

important resource to outwit competitors in the marketplace of management education. Therefore, one comes across catchy glorification of such curricula by management institutions with frequent recourse to superlatives of all kinds. For instance, the IIM Bangalore has so much to boast about its MBA on its website to display the deeply ingrained sense of competition to maintain and enhance its reputation. It projects its programme as revolving around 'the principle that world-class business leaders are not mass-produced; they are nurtured and developed with personalised care and attention, in small work groups and teams, and in a practical, application-oriented user-friendly environment'. It characterises its programme as laying the foundation for conceptual and analytical reasoning while giving the students an insight into the dynamics of the business environment. The programme is geared towards preparing the students to manage and lead in an increasingly complex and dynamic global business scenario. Also, the programme design is inspired by *management practice rather than ivory tower academics* (italics mine). Moreover, it boasts of taking cognisance of the changes *in the social and geo-political scenario that impinge on the management practices* (italics mine).[1]

Interestingly, the mission and vision statements of most of the management institutions in India routinely stress *values* and *social concerns* – the typical justifications for sociology courses in the management curriculum. One of the institutions, the IIM Kozhikode ties up its philosophy of management education to a particular course in sociology as it expects its students to be 'harmonious individuals, socially responsible citizens of tomorrow, in addition to taking up the reins of business and industry'. To this end, it claims a 'delicate blend of management inputs spanning concepts, *social concerns and basic values*'. Moreover, *'the stricture on upholding values is, in fact, brought home to the students' right at the beginning of the programme, when they take a unique, compulsory course on "social transformation in India"'* (all italics mine).[2]

Likewise, *social sensitivity* (and its English language equivalents with minor variations) makes its appearance in the mission and vision statements of almost all management institutions (with minor variations of wordings and changes in emphases). For example, IIM Ahmedabad describes itself as 'a globally respected institute that shapes management practices in India and abroad by creating new frontiers of knowledge and developing ethical, dependable, entrepreneurial, and *socially sensitive* leader managers committed to excellence'. Be that as it may, understandably, sociology occupies almost a tiny place in the overall management curriculum. And this presence is also because of the legacy factor. Institutions where sociology courses have been taught historically are getting pruned, if not banished altogether. The new institutions (for example, a dozen of new IIMs) do not see the need for such courses. Also, management itself has expanded so much in its academic scope and specialisms, that is, there is no room to accommodate related disciplines in its core curriculum. Here and there, there are some generalist courses which may draw on sociology literature. One comes across course titles such as *Contemporary Concerns, Society, Business, and Management, Indian Social and Political Environment, Indian Social Structure, Understanding Contemporary India* in some institutions. But, the overall trend, as indicated earlier, is of decline as new institutions of management have almost stopped recruiting sociologists among their faculty. Even otherwise, as we have discussed in Chapter 2, sociology as a humanist discipline has to struggle hard to find a slot in the crowded timetables and the overburdened workload of the management graduates. A discipline which as accumulated such sobriquets as 'the science of the leftovers', 'the academic custodian of trivialities', 'soft in the centre and fuzzy around the edges', has to swim against the tide.

A sociologist in an Indian institution of management is likely to be part of areas like organisational behaviour (though largely dominated by psychology in India), business environment, marketing, and human resources management. Rural marketing, especially, has scope for sociological research, and in some institutions a few sociologists have successfully changed their professional identity to that of a marketing faculty. Whereas marketing in other countries has seen a definite openness to sociological theories, the same has not been seen in India save few exceptions (Vikas, Varman and Belk 2015; Varman, Goswami and Vijay 2018; Varman and Vijay 2018; Varman and Dholakia 2020). Similarly, organisation studies elsewhere have been the larger institutional home for sociologists, but not so in India where behavioural/psychological perspectives dominate the area (for exceptions see Varman and Saha 2009; Varman, Saha and Skålén 2011; Jammulamadaka 2017, 2019; Vijay and Varman 2017; Vijay 2019). Strategy as an area is almost totally free from the burden of a sociologist's presence in India (much in contrast with elsewhere), even as a few have used sociological frameworks in their research (see Saha 2005; Venkateswaran and Ojha 2017). Indeed, it would be unrealistic to expect much by way of research from sociologists based in institutions of management, given their minuscule presence. The total number of trained sociologists in institutions of management in India would hardly touch the three digits. But the unpalatable aspect of sociologists' presence there comes out clearly in their poor research contributions. Whatever little sociologically informed research has come out of institutions of management, it is more from non-sociologists than sociologists. Clearly, there is a problem of scale given the abysmally low strength of sociologists in institutions of management. But the bigger constraint is that of the peculiarity of sociological practices in India. Indian sociology lacks a healthy and robust tradition of sociological investigation in the industrial and corporate sectors, notwithstanding the sub-discipline of industrial sociology. Surprisingly, even today, there is no accessible text or research literature on the increasingly influential Indian managerial class. What you have are indeed coffee table books with some biographies thrown in. Except for the studies of trade unions or labour relations and a few descriptive ethnographies of particular industrial settings, sociologists appear to have missed the opportunity to contribute to some of the frontier areas of research. One notices similar dearth of literature on the theme of sociology of consumption in India. In the following section, we discuss this rather weak tradition of sociologically studying 'the economic' in India. This has led to such a weak foundation of economic sociology in our country.

More importantly, a sociologist does not have something readymade to offer to the short-duration Management Development Programmes (MDPs). Through convention, themes such as leadership, conflict, and negotiation have come to become the naturalised preserve of OB professionals. A sociologist has to either get into this disciplinary turf war or think of something innovative which may not have an easy market acceptance. Its failure on this count – the failure to organise training programmes and to offer consultancy to the corporate sector – further pushes it down in the institutional hierarchy in terms of relevance. Even when sociologists are increasingly getting involved in NGOs, consultancies, corporate research, social impact assessment, and social auditing, the public image of sociology as an esoteric discipline dealing with worn-out themes like caste and village continues to discourage such efforts. As we will see in the following section, sociologists in institutions of management are rather ill-equipped to perform the tasks expected of them. If their research contributions are poor, it is not because they lack initiative or drive or are ill-disposed towards research, but because they are ill-equipped to work in interdisciplinary contexts given their training. This question does not belong to the domain of psychology. It is a sociological question. And, that is why it is important to situate this question in the larger framework of disciplinary history and professional socialisation.

Most of the sociologists come from Indian universities which have institutionalised a particular understanding of sociology. The dominant ethos of the discipline generates a 'trained incapacity' to practice sociology in non-university settings like institutions of management. Generations of students have been brought up on a heavy dose of Nisbet's (1976) *sociology as an art form* and Bottomore's (1974) *sociology as social criticism* which have disseminated the idea of sociology as a critical humanising discipline. They have been taught to glorify the debunking motif of sociology and mount mechanical critique of positivism and structural-functionalism without ever getting exposed to the serious positivist traditions of sociological research. They have learnt to be apologetic about sociology's meagre accomplishments in terms of offering feasible solutions to real-life problems. They have been taught the subtle intricacies of conceptual distinctions between a social problem and a sociological problem – the latter being the ideal disciplinary provenance. *The dominant disciplinary culture has communicated to them in so many ways that the more removed a sociologist is from the real world of everyday, the greater a sociologist she is.* An implied distinction between theoretical Brahmins and empirical Shudras in relation to internal division of labour within Indian sociology appears to have been at work.

In institutions of management, where inter-disciplinary collaboration is necessitated by the sheer lack of a critical number of peers in sociology (and where many others may be ignorant of, or simply indifferent to, sociology), the mainstream disciplinary training and professional socialisation do act as added constraints on a sociologist's ability of productive adaptation to the challenging environment of a professional institution, and her agility to go for fruitful inter-disciplinary collaboration on a relevant problem, business or otherwise. The disciplinary mainstream in India has failed to appreciate the need for rounded training to students of sociology so that they can bring in their expertise to optimal use in varied institutional contexts. Regrettably, much of the training remains oriented towards producing teachers of sociology in conventional colleges and universities without any serious consideration of multiple demands being made on the discipline by various stakeholders. One finds this lack of appreciation in the various reports periodically produced under the auspices of the UGC and the ICSSR. Also, the persistence of the university-ordained monochromatic understanding of sociology can be discerned in the activities and organisation of the Indian Sociological Society – the supreme professional body of sociologists in the country.

The roots of this particular professional socialisation go much deeper and are predicated upon the ingrained asymmetrical assessment of theoretical and applied research in general. To some extent, it is related to the very nature of university as an institution. Citing Clark Kerr, Lipset (1982) observes that even as academics persistently support local and national social change efforts they take an opposite stance when the academy itself is the focus of concern. According to Lipset (1982: 156), 'Few institutions are so conservative as universities about their own affairs. While their members are so liberal about the affairs of others, the more elite the professor, the more liberal he or she is on social issues; but the opposite holds on matters that affect the academy'. Even otherwise, 'the bottom line', to use the management jargon, 'is that life at the border of sociology and management is not for everyone. It is a comfortable location only if you are willing to move beyond the boundaries of sociology, and at the same time, are inclined to bring sociological ideas into management' (Meyer 1999: 509–10). It is not that sociology can solve problems or offer any ready-made answers to the challenges of our times. However, one needs to stress that engagement in applied research does not automatically amount to the undermining of the discipline's self-reflexivity.

Also, it should be stressed that applied sociological research does not necessarily mean a less rigorous engagement with the discipline. Heuristically speaking, as DeMartini (1983) argues, there are two types of applied sociology. One tradition of work emphasises the utilisation of the basic empirical methods of the discipline in collecting and gathering information needed to make informed decisions or opinions on matters of practical concern. Evaluation research, programme evaluation, cost–benefit analysis and social impact assessment, public opinion polling, market analysis, and community ethnography belong to this genre of work which finds its organisational expressions in entities such as ACNielsen ORG-MARG, Microsoft, and numerous research and advocacy NGOs. The other kind of work utilises the discipline's concepts in interpreting relevant data and hopefully in providing a more accurate understanding of social determinants and the possible outcome of proposed social action. Analysis of social problems and policy research and analysis would fit in this variety of applied research. Thus, there exists a vast field where sociology can potentially contribute by way of applied and problem-oriented policy research.

However, very often, the pursuit of applied research is seen as a threat to the integrity of the discipline. It is seen as undermining the critical core of the discipline. Conventional sociologists ensconced in the prestigious (and the not-so-prestigious) university departments may find it challenging to move out of their comfort zones that the habitual world of repetitive courses and disciplined classrooms, familiar bodies of literature, do-it-easy research method textbooks, and secure work environments have secured for them. Given this, to conceive of a change in the institutional setting of their disciplinary practices is not only unattractive but also fraught with unnecessary risk. In institutions of management, sociologists are per force engaged in an everyday act of communication of what sociology is all about as they confront their multi-disciplinary colleagues, academic administrators, students, and the general public who have pretty vague ideas (or no idea altogether) about what sociologists do. Such a communication may not be totally absent from a university either. But surely, the degrees vary and a university sociologist can bask in the glory of her department or faculty which may have a certain historical depth. In the latter setting, the legitimacy of sociology as an academic discipline need not be argued out on an everyday basis. Sociologists in professional institutions have to continually think of novel ways to make their discipline institutionally relevant, a burden that university sociologists are free from. In doing so, the former contributes to the expansion and re-calibration of the disciplinary domain and also helps enlarge the disciplinary scope by employing sociological perspectives and methods to new areas.

It is a moot point if extending the scope of the discipline through applied research is a better professional strategy – something that sociologists in the United Kingdom have taken recourse to. The other option is to keep rueing the decline in the state support for social sciences, commercialisation of higher education, the general decline in the prestige of liberal education, and the public image of sociology as an academic discipline. For example, Freeman and Rossi (1984) convincingly demonstrate how applied work could mitigate the consequences of the shrinking opportunities for sociologists in the academic labour market. But then, applied sociology continues to have negative associations. In the Indian context, it lacks an image altogether, or at best, has an ambivalent positioning within the mainstream professional establishment. The fear of getting bogged down by applied interests led the professional leaders of the yore to claim an exclusive space for knowledge producing activity of the academic kind (see Thakur 2006). As a corollary, it also meant keeping away promising sociologists from such applied interests despite expanding job opportunities in non-university and non-academic settings.

The peculiarities of Indian sociology

Like elsewhere, sociology in India has acquired certain local attributes owing to the historical specificities of its growth and development as an academic discipline. These peculiarities have imparted it with an orientation which has made it less hospitable towards a serious disciplinary engagement with the 'economic'. In fact, a cursory glance at the century-old history of Indian sociology reveals its relative under-engagement with economic phenomena and processes. Although the 'economic' did get studied under the influence of agrarian and village studies, and certain apparently economic themes like industry and labour did attract scholarly attention from some sociologists, there has been a noticeable absence of a sustained and robust academic tradition of sociological studies of the economy in India. There appears to have been an intellectual division of labour where the study of economic issues was ceded to economists, whereas sociologists remained jubilant with their studies of traditional institutions of caste, village, family, and the like. In what follows, we present a brief discussion of this persistent disjunction between the social and the economic, which has had implications for the place of sociology in management education.

Indeed, Indian sociology, as conceptualised and executed by its dominant mainstream, never fancied itself as a policy science or a problem-oriented discipline with applied orientation. Its projected image has been that of a critical discipline, incapable, and mostly unwilling, to offer any quick-fix remedies to the innumerable problems facing the country and society (Srinivas and Panini 1973). Save a few exceptions, it did not make assertive claims on matters of public policy, and therefore, was not seen as a policy-relevant applied social science with any immediate pay-offs to the enterprise of nation-building. Surely, Indian sociology seemed to be at odds with the requirements of the national state (Deshpande 2018). The biggest political challenge of the time was to unify a society ravaged by colonialism and religion-based partition and to build a 'casteless and classless society' (Srinivas 1994: 14).

In the immediate aftermath of Independence, India also witnessed various secessionist movements and language-based mobilizations. Amidst such a divisive context, sociology's preoccupation with the fault-lines of Indian society – caste, religion, gender, and ethnicity – did not serve its public image well. It came to be seen as a discipline preoccupied with institutional remnants of the past. Such documentation of these changing institutions was indifferently tolerated under the confidence that they were bound to disappear under India's tryst with development and modernity. In any case, sociology, unlike economics, was not seen as making any lasting contribution to the lofty goal of national development. This was also because of its focus and theoretical and methodological resources that were available to the discipline. Since much of its mainstream scholarship was geared towards understanding the basic working of India's traditional institutions, sociology's ability to frame effective policy solutions to even social problems remained suspect. Additionally, there was a widespread belief that economic development, once it gained momentum, would address most of the problems, including the social ones. Little wonder, the seemingly ideologically neutral and techno-scientific language of economics held such a sway among the political class and policymakers.

Besides, sociology in India has never been sociology *per se* as the term has been understood elsewhere. Given its peculiar historicity of growth and development Indian sociology has, in effect, been social anthropology *tout court*. While a difference between the two exists elsewhere, in India, it is social anthropology that is practiced under the disciplinary label of sociology (Deshpande 2018). Sociology emerged out of colonial social anthropology in colonial India, and it has carried its birthmarks till the present. Eventually, after India's Independence, much of social anthropology underwent a change in nomenclature and overnight turned into sociology without any significant change in the disciplinary practices. In terms of substantive themes and methodological approaches social anthropology keeps masquerading as sociology even today with marginal sociological theories thrown in. It would not be an exaggeration to assert that Indian sociology has been but rebranded social anthropology (Béteille 2013).

There is no need to belabour the point that most influential sociologists in India have been trained social anthropologists, and they did not want sociology to be subservient to the state or the idea of policy relevance. Instead, at least aspirationally, their scholarly concern was to develop a theoretical construction of Indian society and to find out the most appropriate sociological paradigm for its study (Thapan 1998). A strand of thinking held the view that sociology in India should be primarily concerned with the Hindu society and its institutional structures and practices. Dumont and Pocock (1957: 7), for example, argued that 'a sociology of India lies at the point of confluence of Sociology and Indology', and insisted on the need to study Indian culture and tradition through classical (Sanskrit) textual sources.

Against this 'book-view' of Indian society, M. N. Srinivas, the most influential Indian sociologist, advocated the 'field-based' research in Indian sociology. Srinivas believed that village represented the microcosm of Indian social life and only ethnographic fieldwork, based on overt 'participant observation', could adequately capture the nuances of it – including the radical transformation that India was going through (Srinivas 1994). For him, the fieldwork offered a rich repertoire of tools to discover the hidden, unfamiliar, and systematic in one's own society or the 'other' (Béteille 2013). This determination of Srinivas and his followers to set up Indian sociology on the foundations of the ethnographic field work became the defining characteristic of the discipline. This fieldwork-based social anthropological approach stood in stark contrast to the methodology popularised by American sociology – that of survey-based research, using questionnaires and the opinion-based polls (Patel 1998). Admittedly, when sociology elsewhere maintained methodological flexibility (which included enough room for quantitative research as well), sociology in India became exclusively identified with the fieldwork-oriented micro studies. This considerably reduced its elbow room to engage in meaningful conversations with quantitatively oriented disciplines employing survey-based research and mathematical/statistical tools.

For Indian sociology, the study of 'the village community' became the most influential stock-in-trade (Thakur 2014a). Sociological research works primarily focused on aspects of caste, kinship, gender, family, and religion in the empirical setting of a village. Not only was the village the grand empirical and conceptual pivot for Indian sociology, but caste also became, as Saberwal (1982: 44) put it, the 'private obsession' of Indian sociologists. This preference for the study of 'traditional' institutions through ethnographic fieldwork through participant observation became the constitutive core of the discipline. Little wonder, despite much ado about 'comparative method', sociology remained anchored in the narrow grooves of community studies, and thus, its methodological particularism distanced it from other social sciences. For instance, as noted earlier, sociology failed to sustain a serious scholarly interest in the study of economic issues despite the fact that some of its pioneers in India were trained economists. In fact, some of them maintained a keen interest in economic issues. They not only directly engaged with various economic phenomena and processes but also critically analysed the methodology of mainstream (neoclassical) economics. It is no coincidence that Radhakamal Mukerjee, one of the founding fathers of sociology in India, pioneered the institutionalist tradition in Indian economic thinking. He proudly carried the title of 'professor of economics and sociology' at Lucknow University for decades (Thakur 2014b). He argued about the absence of a theory of institutions in mainstream Indian economics. He believed that the problem-solving skills of economics could be fully harnessed only when it went beyond the abstract notion of *Homo economicus* and utilitarian thinking and took into consideration other factors which are socially determined.

In a similar vein, Mukerji (1958: 53) criticized the reckless generalization characteristic of economics and called for the need to understand economic issues 'in the light of local actualities, including tradition, institution, myths, beliefs, ideas, and symbols'. In fact, Mukerji encouraged students to treat economics as a cultural subject. For him, policy solutions to concrete economic problems needed to start from the concrete reality of Indian social structure. Seen thus, some of these writings did stress the embeddedness of the 'economic' in the 'social' and did not turn away from the need to integrate the 'social' and 'the economic' in a unifying framework. This kind of sociological scholarship which underlined the need for a conscious synthesis of theory and methods spanning both economics and sociology for a critical appreciation of the historical specificity of Indian socio-cultural reality was soon overshadowed by the Srinivasian variety of culturalist studies of little communities in the country.

Moreover, some of these pioneers were the early advocates what we now call inter-disciplinarity. Mukerji opined that a capable and fruitful social science could only be achieved when one transcended the artificial disciplinary boundaries and focused on theorizing the reality as it was. Such openness to disciplinary boundaries made it possible for Mukerji to head a department of economics at the Aligarh Muslim University (AMU) after a long stint as a teacher of sociology at the University of Lucknow. Likewise, Patrick Geddes, the founder of the oldest sociology department in Mumbai, was an avowed town planner and had an abiding interest in cities and human ecology. G.S. Ghurye, Geddes's successor in Mumbai, was not averse to the study of economic issues of contemporary significance. Admittedly, Ghurye's own work on the subject is less voluminous compared to Lucknow sociologists, and his students did engage with the economic phenomena of sociological consequence. It is safe to assert that, for the founding fathers of Indian sociology, the economic was hardly a no-go area, and some of them thought seriously about inter-disciplinarity, or even a trans-disciplinary social science (Mukerjee 1960).

In subsequent years, as discussed in the foregoing, Indian sociology started charting out a path that would take it away from serious studies of economic themes and issues. As a consequence, the study of the economic domain became the sole and legitimate preserve of economists. And, the generous and the sensitive among the latter would accommodate, and occasionally encourage, sociologists to fill in the assigned slots as analysts of cultural aspects of economic growth and development. This reduced engagement with economic issues almost became a disciplinary norm for Indian sociologists. Instead, the village studies came to stand for Indian sociology, which further evolved as a study of inter-caste relations (community studies) in the empirical setting of a village. Among those who undertook village studies, very few (Dube 1958; Joshi 1969; Epstein 1973; Bliss and Stern 1982) effectively focused on economic issues such as the land question, land reforms, agricultural transformation, economic development, occupational mobility, and the like.

In the mid-1960s, some sociologists did turn their attention towards industrial workers in India. Their writings were mainly directed as an empirical response to a group of American-based scholars. The latter argued that the workers in developing countries, where industrialization was gathering pace, were, in fact, hampering the process due to their inability – owing to the influence of traditional, sociocultural forces – to adjust to the industrial way of life (Bhowmik 2009). While this came out as a general observation, the subsequent studies carried out by sociologists resulted in contesting claims (Sharma 1974; Holmström 1976). Evidently, the role of primordial loyalties – based on caste, religion, family, kinship, and ethnicity – within factory settings and the nature of industrial conflict received attention in such studies (see Ramaswamy and Sheth 1968; Ramaswamy 1981; Parry 1999). Concomitantly, issues related to labour started gaining scholarly attention. The studies that followed focused on themes such as the informal nature of the Indian economy, workers' identity and resistance, alienation, workers' skill (Sharma 1974; Sheth 1977), and living conditions and job satisfaction of workers (Gani 1991). Besides, the activities of trade unions garnered some attention. N. R. Sheth's (1996) study looked at the effectiveness of trade unions in a changing socio-economic environment in India. There have been studies of 'footloose labour' by Jan Breman (1996). Such works cumulatively constitute the sub-disciplinary fields of industrial sociology and sociology of labour.

However, as Surendran (2018: 127) rightly asserts, 'except for a few honourable exceptions, the body of work that constitutes the corpus of industrial sociology has largely been undertaken in periods of fleeting or nomadic interest by scholars, at best as their subsidiary inclination'. The predominant focus remained caste, and as Morris (1965) writes, 'those who have studied caste have ignored industry, and those who have studied industry ignored caste'. As a consequence, industrial sociology could never emerge as a vibrant field of study. It remained restrictive in its scope and did not encourage sociological studies of themes like industrial neighbourhood, spatial character of manufacturing and production, and the every day in an industrial setting with all its attendant complexities. Whatever few studies that have been there restricted the study of industrial life to organisation, interest, conflict, and industrial relations (Surendran 2018). And such studies did not go on to contribute to the robustness of the fledgling field of sociology of organisations (Chaturvedi and Chaturvedi 1995). Our argument has been that this weak growth of the above-mentioned disciplinary fields is an outcome of Indian sociology's long-lasting reluctance to explore the 'economic' in its varied historical and contemporary dimensions.

In short, while sociologists in India did engage with economic themes and issues, to begin with, the tradition lost momentum because of the ascendancy of a particular type of sociology under the influence of M.N. Srinivas and his social anthropological moorings. These disciplinary specificities undermined the research abilities and professional development of generations of students who were not encouraged to explore the applied kind of sociological research. This is at the root of what we have earlier characterised as 'trained incapacity' of sociologists to ably function in the context of professional institutions including management. Sociology can very well be both a perspective-building critical discipline given to the understanding of social processes and phenomena shaping the context we live in and an empirical discipline engaged in applied, problem-driven, and policy-relevant research. It does not help to keep lamenting the way Marshall W. Meyer (1999: 508) of the well-known Wharton Business School, University of Pennsylvania, does, 'the sociological perspective which emphasises the role of values, institutions and social structures in human behaviour is not fully appreciated and may never be'.

Conclusion

In this chapter, we have tried to argue that the place of sociology in management education has been a function of both the changing conceptualisation of management as an academic discipline (and its implications for the perceived role and legitimacy of related disciplines in the institutions of management) and the particular national history of sociology (the way its disciplinary mainstream has been shaped professionally in the country and its implications for the public legitimacy of sociology in relation to other disciplines). In particular, sociology gets discounted in the context of management education because of both –the particularities of the discipline and the institutional context wherein it wishes to mark its presence.

On a different plane, there is the need for the simple realisation that practices of an academic discipline differ institutionally. Doing sociology in an institution of management is qualitatively different from doing it in a university. Regrettably, there has been fitful dialogue among practitioners of sociology across the institutional divide. We need to create more spaces for empathetic and thoughtful dialogue among them to dislodge the current tendency wherein university sociologists look upon those working in professional institutions, and *vice versa*. Viewed thus, claiming a legitimate space for sociology in a management institution is as much an internal struggle as an external one. The calling of sociology calls for consistent renewal and persistent interpretation of the critical gaze, including the turning of that gaze on disciplinary practices themselves. The existence of different 'publics' (Burawoy 2016), as the fashionable term goes, necessitates continual re-calibration of sociological knowledge, perspectives, and practices depending on the available audience.

In the next chapter, we examine the intertwined roles of the changed institutional contexts and audiences in the making of critical management studies (CMS). We chart out its origins in the general context of management studies with a particular focus on the role of sociology in its emergence and growth. The next chapter chronicles the much-debated trajectory of the CMS and brings out its political, institutional, and disciplinary imperatives. The chapter also attempts to explore and contextualise the possibility of the growth of CMS in the context of management studies in India.

Notes

1. www.iimb.ac.in accessed on 12 August 2020.
2. www.iimk.ac.in accessed on 12 August 2020.

4 Privileging critique
Sociology and its metamorphosis into critical management studies

Introduction: disciplinary/institutional traffic and its after-effects

This chapter presents a detailed discussion of critical management studies (CMS). It outlines the context of its emergence and assesses its impact on the contemporary practices of management education and research. CMS has emerged as a fundamental critique of conventional management studies and carries with it an aura of novelty and radicalism. As an emerging field, it is increasingly attracting management academics in the English-speaking world. The chapter traces the theoretical, ideological, and methodological genealogies of CMS amidst an array of political discontents that surfaced in the 1960s and thereafter. This chapter offers a critique of CMS as well and hints at its possible futures in the context of its uncomfortable relationship with mainstream institutions and practices of management.

Even as academic disciplines embody distinctive forms of knowledge, they are hardly immune from the effects of their institutional locales or the organisational milieus in which they work out their everyday practices. As we have seen in earlier chapters, doing sociology in a university department cannot be compared to practising it in an institution of management or in a business school. These qualitative differences emanating from different institutional settings lead not only to the divergent understanding of an academic discipline but also to the varied self-image of their professional practitioners and their altering engagements with the discipline. For example, what would generally be seen as sociology of work, employment, and organisation in a university setting turns out to be interlinked academic modules on organisational behaviour and human resources management in a business school. In this sense, the institutional context of the practices of a discipline deserves as much consideration as the internal theoretical and methodological developments. In effect, the two have been inextricably linked. That is why, in our framework employed in this book, we have veered towards sociology of knowledge approach than being merely reliant on an abstract philosophy of science approach. A paradigm shift in a discipline has greater anchorage in the practices of the scientific (disciplinary) community concerned than the self-propelled autonomous march of ideas and frameworks (Kuhn 1962). For the limited purpose of this book, nothing illustrates this better than the emergence and growing ascendance of CMS in the context of management studies.

CMS emerged as a self-identifiable group of primarily British scholars (with some scholars from countries like Australia and New Zealand, and later the United States and Canada) in the early 1990s who self-consciously embarked on questioning the fundamental assumptions of what they considered to be the mainstream management education and research. They wanted to do serious onion-peeling of the scholarly practices, writings, and teaching of the ones located in management institutions: whose interests are being promoted by such scholarly and institutional practices, and whose interests are being sacrificed, side-lined, overlooked by the extant practices of management and research. According to CMS scholars, related disciplines of management like industrial sociology and psychology, along with management, have been preoccupied with the optimisation of labour productivity right from the days of the Hawthorne experiments. This has been evident in the disproportionate amount of research around labour commitment theory and other aspects of human relations approach (Sodhi and Plowman 2002). The latter has been geared towards increasing workers' efficiency and enhancing managerial control (Thompson 2011). There has been no serious attempt to see the linkages between the increases in workers' efficiency and the disproportionate financial benefits to the owners of capital. In fact, management, as a discipline, provides an ideological justification to the practice of the incessant milking of the hapless workers for the ever-greater profit. The mainstream management studies, in fact, chose not to look at the manipulative and the exploitative side of human relations school of Elton Mayo of the Hawthorne studies fame (Bruce and Nyland 2011).

Their endeavour has always been to make workers more and more understanding of the managerial superiority and of cloaking the interests of the capitalists in the name of efficiency and productivity. CMS constituted itself in opposition to what it considered to be the widely prevalent uncritical and unthinking pro-management approach of the management scholars. It saw itself as the carrier of sociology's traditionally critical approach to management institutions. It carried the self-image of a group of serious scholars interested in going deeper into underlying causes of organisational phenomena, which most management scholars study only superficially. In a way, CMS conceived itself as an oppositional movement whose significant other was the mainstream management education (Hancock 2008).

By the mid-1990s, CMS successfully established itself as a sub-disciplinary field with its own conferences, journals, and other insignia of relative autonomy from the general field of management studies. However, CMS is not the same as sociology, even as it has drawn overwhelmingly from sociology – 'its most obvious parent' (Parker 2014: 169). In a related way, CMS is not totally immersed in the landscape of the business school. Neither sociology nor management, the CMS evolved into something new – a generic though hybrid area of study. Yet, as we will see in this chapter, the growth of CMS has considerable implications for sociology and other related social science disciplines within business schools. While drawing upon foundational disciplines like sociology, CMS has turned out to be the progenitor of a new type of scholarly work in the context of management education, which has made post-structuralism and post-modernism the legitimate theoretical medium of scholarly conversation in terms of culturalist tropes of meaning, subjectivity, identity, and reflexivity (Vaara 2011). The growing popularity of CMS in the organisational-institutional context of management education has also made it the target of various attacks for its feigned political radicalism. In the words of Parker (2013: 170): 'Indeed, the restless reflexivity and theoretical neophilia which is characteristic of CMS could easily be understood as a recipe for political quietism which masquerades as intellectual radicalism'.

It is too early to speculate on the future of CMS in the institutions of management. What it has surely succeeded in doing is too see management as part of the larger complex of contemporary capitalism. However, CMS itself, as the following discussion shows, is not a homogeneous field. There are competing strands of thinking within the field, with the predominant being oriented towards a discursive reading of capitalism as an ideological and cultural phenomenon borne out of Foucauldian influences (Parush 2008). Of course, there still are adherents to the Braverman's 'Labour Process Theory' (LPT) within the same fold of CMS. Also, there are those who are increasingly uncomfortable with CMS as a superficial critique of the capitalist ideology but ultimately contributing to the reproduction of the status quo. By now, there is considerable literature on CMS. There is also almost a consensual understanding that CMS derives its distinctive historicity from the British experience.

Privileging critique 71

In institutional terms, it is the result of the simultaneous shrinking of sociology departments in British universities and the growth of the business schools in the United Kingdom from the 1980s onwards. This institutional traffic was the initial condition for the emergence of CMS. As 'the labour market for sociologists to teach in their "home" departments was shrinking', they were compelled to move to medical faculties; social work and policy departments; schools of education, criminology, and development studies. But for these academic émigrés, as Parker notes, the most congenial institutional home came by way of the expanding institutions of management: 'But by far the biggest demand was from the "organizational behaviour" parts of business schools that needed a labour force to teach "people and organisations" core courses as part of the curriculum' (Parker 2013: 166). Expectedly, during this institutional transition things did not remain the same: 'Of course, as things travel, so do they change, because that which arrived in the business school was not the same as that which left sociology' (Parker 2013: 163).

The academic commitments of the sociologists in their new institutional locales came to be shaped differently and not necessarily by the sociology that they left behind. The interplay of the emergence of CMS in business schools owing to its inspiration from sociology as a critical discipline and sociology's almost simultaneous institutional decline (at least in the United Kingdom) has fuelled an interminable debate (Reed 1985; Scott 2005; Holmwood 2010; Savage 2010; Beynon 2011; Cooper 2012). This British experience gradually percolated to the other English-speaking countries, finally reaching the Academy of Management in the United States. However, it is only appropriate to underline the fact that the huge influence of the growth of CMS has barely reached the Indian shores. Indeed, a small group of Indian scholars are active interlocutors in the field of CMS in terms of their publications and/or their enthusiastic participation in the activities of the CMS Division of the Academy of Management (AOM) (Varman and Saha 2009; Varman, Saha and Skålén 2011; Jammulamadaka 2017, 2019; Vijay and Varman 2017; Vijay 2019).

In the Indian context, academic socialisation in the field of management education has been led by the Indian Institute of Management (IIM) system modelled as stand-alone institutions. Not only is academic socialisation of an IIM of a different order compared to a university, but it has also been substantially internal to the system. In the United States and the United Kingdom, many prestigious management schools/institutions, departments are part of the University system. And we have repeatedly talked about the scale of interaction between social science departments like sociology and management institutions. In India, these interactions remained far from acquiring any critical mass in terms of institutional/disciplinary traffic whereas, as we would see below, the scale of these interactions in the United Kingdom led to the novelty of CMS as an intellectual field in its own right.

The 'novelty' of CMS: recasting critical theory and beyond

Undoubtedly, the entry of a large number of sociologists into the institutions of management triggered the intellectual formation that we now designate as CMS. But it was not just the arrival of sociology onto the management landscape that offers the complete answer. According to Parker (2014: 173), one has to look into the type of sociologists who moved to the business schools. Most of them were a disgruntled lot having a sense of estrangement with the disciplinary practices of mainstream sociology. These sociologists moved from sociology at a time when sociology itself had become an intellectual home for a variety of countercultural currents of Marxism, feminism, critical theory, and post-structuralism. For such radical sociologists, anything managerial would appear as proverbial red rag to a bull. They wanted a gradual re-description, and an eventual overhaul, of what management education was all about. They saw that complexities of human action are getting reduced to behaving in organisations in business schools.

Likewise, they found a unitarist social psychology characteristic of the human relations school informing the discourse of human resources management in mainstream management education. To their surprise, questions of culture, leadership, change, and structure were approached as if there were no politics to knowledge. In the mainstream discourse they were bewildered to see a complete lack of sensitivity to the unequal control of resources and the uneven distribution of rewards. They were at a loss to explain the gradual replacement of the studies of trade unions and collective bargaining by the 'cow sociology' of personnel and HRM.[1] CMS scholars accused the sociologists working in institutions of management as the inheritors of a human relations account of adjustment to the workplace and thus unduly preoccupied with the focus on worker's motivations and commitment, orientations to work, and the like. In their reading, 'the sociologist then ... is not seen as the inheritor of a critical tradition at all, but an arriviste stooge for the bosses whose job is to ensure that happy cows produce more milk' (Parker 2013: 167).

Scholars belonging to CMS classification wanted to revitalise what they found to be a social psychology-driven, intellectually unchallenging, and politically sterile field of conventional management education. For this, they drew heavily on non-management thought, which definitely gave a certain vibrancy to CMS in its formative years. Its tireless focus on the need for the immanent critique of the field of management education *tout court* breathed in a fresh air of intellectual sophistication and political savviness to an otherwise atheoretical and academically flat landscape. Such a reading of the institutional landscape of the conventional management education galvanised a group of émigré scholars to start with a special interest group, which subsequently managed to become a division at the AOM. This institutionalisation as a sub-disciplinary area witnessed the range of activities characteristic of any new intellectual movement: critical articles, programmatic statements, parallel associations and conferences, readers and resource books (Alvesson and Willmott 1992a, 1992b, 1992c, 2003, 2008, 2011, 2012; Grey and Willmott 2005). It is appropriate to begin with the official statement of CMS that is there on the AOM website:

> Our premise is that structural features of contemporary society such as profit imperative, patriarchy, racial inequality, and ecological irresponsibility often turn organisations into instruments of domination and exploitation. Driven by a shared desire to change this situation, we aim in our research teaching and practice, to develop critical interpretation of management and society and to generate radical alternatives. Our critique seeks to connect the practical shortcomings in management and individual managers to the demands of a socially divisive and ecologically destructive system within which individual managers work.

The above-mentioned fragment of the programmatic statement evidently reveals both the wide scope of CMS and its sociological flavour. The critique encompasses the whole of society and not merely individuals, firms, and organisations. For CMS, the agenda of the conventional management studies is politically driven rather than scientifically motivated. The latter refuses to look at the darker side of contemporary capitalism. By contrast, CMS is often accused of going to the extent of muckraking with an inventory of worst practices of capitalism. In fact, CMS academics' charge against the conventional management studies is that it only brings to light the cases showing the best practices. In any case, the plea that the mainstream management focuses on larger issues goes well with the disciplinary imperatives of sociology, which (compared to psychology) has historically shown greater sensitivity to the larger social context of human action. In a manner of speaking, CMS is primarily defined as an intellectual counter-movement to the conventional management studies.

Evidently, both the terms have witnessed a range of interpretations and have been attributed characteristics based on the ideological/theoretical predilections of the interpreter. One of the most influential attempts to outline the epistemic virtues of CMS against the conventional management studies has been that of Fournier and Grey (2000). Delineating the conditions and prospects for critical scholarship in the business schools, Fournier and Grey (2000) underline three cardinal attributes of CMS: non-performativity, denaturalisation, and reflexivity. To the extent that CMS do not intend to improve the effectiveness of managerial practice for gains in productivity or increase the efficiency of organizational processes, it can be seen as characterized by an ethos of *non-performativity*. Unlike conventional management studies, CMS purposely and steadfastly wish to transgress 'a means-ends calculation' (Fournier and Grey 2000: 17).

Against this narrow profit imperative which remains the defining feature of conventional management scholarship, CMS bring out issues around power, domination, control and inequality that constitute work and workplaces under capitalism. In order to achieve this objective, CMS adopts the strategy and ethos of *denaturalization* whereby CMS scholars do not accept management knowledge at its face value but actively seek to historicise, expose, and challenge its ideological underpinnings. This amounts to unpacking those processes of knowledge production which have rendered the motifs of stakeholder's value or profit as naturalised constructs. The process of denaturalisation is equally meant to bring to the fore alternative values and frameworks that have been pushed to the background by dominant forms of knowledge and their organizational and institutional outcomes.

The most trumpeted attribute of CMS is its inherent *reflexivity*. It has become almost axiomatic that the CMS scholars tend to reflect on their epistemological, ontological and methodological assumptions far more explicitly than their mainstream counterparts (Eden 2003). For them, the scientific neutrality or disinterestedness of academic research is a positivist cloak discouraging researchers to look at their own situatedness in the research process. This suggests that CMS scholars take the socially constructed and politically contested nature of knowledge as their point of departure, and seldom hesitate to mount their reflexive gaze on their own scholarly practices (Ford, Harding and Learmonth 2010). The principal function of CMS is to demonstrate the ways in which management has come to acquire a key organizational function and an indispensable identity as an occupational group. This taken-for-grantedness of the centrality of management is to be questioned and is to be positioned as a construction which came into existence through a series of historical moves separating it from other activities and occupations. In this sense, the supremacy of managerial work is not a naturally given imperative but the outcome of the transformations in the nature and meaning of managerial work under capitalist organization of production.

Seen thus, CMS is not the critique of contemporary workplace practices alone. Rather, it is the fundamental critique of the philosophical and political basis of management and the ideological work it has historically done, and is doing. In other words, the mandate of CMS turns out to be retrieving the lost voice and forced silence in the context of business schools to render the latter thoroughly critical institutions. It amounts to pitting a new type of ideological mission to the current ones championed by the business schools (Grey 2002: 505). To this extent, the CMS entails a degree of courage on the part of its proponents, it means both a rejection of orthodox approaches as well as continual engagement with them for the latter rules the roost. Though simplistic, the following box brings out the key differences between conventional and CMS:

Conventional Management Studies	Critical Management Studies
Narrow focus on business and profit	Broader focus on social justice and ecological sustainability
Concerned with the maximisation of shareholders' interests	Concerned with stakeholders' value; society being an important stakeholder
Ethos characterised by the Milton Friedman's dictum of business of business is business	Ethos shaped by the social responsibility of business and its larger ethical concerns for human welfare, dignity, non-discrimination
Profit maximisation is the key goal	Universal emancipation is the key goal
Theoretical inspiration from thinkers like Frederick Winslow Taylor, Henry Fayol, Henry Ford	Theoretical inspiration from Theodor Adorno, Jurgen Habermas, Max Horkheimer, Herbert Marcuse, Michel Foucault
Quantitative-scientific methodological protocols	Hermeneutic-interpretive methodological protocols
Theoretical generalisation as a science	Reflexive micro-narratives
Faith in Enlightenment ideals like science, progress, development, reason	Disenchantment with Enlightenment ideals, celebration of the fragment
Positivist in orientation	Post-modernist and post-structuralist in orientation
Value-neutrality in teaching and research	Critical academic praxis
Productive endeavour to improve capitalism as a system through efficiency and inclusiveness	Continual critique of capitalism as an inegalitarian and unjust system

76 *Privileging critique*

To instil critical questioning in an inhospitable terrain like business schools means doing much more than launching a tirade against the defects of global capitalism or presenting a list of misdeeds of capitalist organizations. Of course, documenting and disclosing various kinds of sweatshop experiences is important as it reveals some of the dynamics of power and control in the workplace. This *per force* means questioning the tidy textbook account of organizations current in orthodox management studies, which projects all problems as mere technical problems calling for technical solutions.

CMS does not look at a managerial or organizational problem in terms of technical solutions alone. Rather, it focuses on the social relations surrounding an apparently technical problem. The overall objective is to develop an understanding of the complexities of managerial interaction and control. Evidently, CMS, the way its proponents see it, is much more than the simple addition of 'critical' as an adjectival prefix to the existing topics in the curriculum or the set of research questions. It is about de-legitimatizing the unstated assumptions of the orthodox management scholarship. For example, key concepts like market relations and managerial dominance as normal and natural features of social organization need to be interrogated. Likewise, the idea of management as an ideology-free technique and practice needs to be debunked and the linkages between the changing conceptions of the market and enterprise in the wider society and the ascendance of mainstream management scholarship need to be probed.

Almost all CMS scholars work in management institutions and they have to continually engage with the mainstream of the business schools in their work as teachers, researchers, and practitioners. Admittedly, CMS exists in those very institutions whose critique has been its *raison d'etre*. CMS scholars have been enacting the role of the critical insiders from within, rather than from outside, the portals of the business schools. Indeed, CMS exists within certain pockets of business schools despite having attained the status of a division within the American Academy of Management which has certainly raised its profile of in North America. Nevertheless, it remains most visible within the United Kingdom, Scandinavia, Australia, and New Zealand. Moreover, CMS academics are not part of all the institutions of management even within these countries. Nor are they necessarily represented in typically the most prestigious of institutions in terms of international ranking systems and accreditation. To a large extent, CMS is concentrated within the organization studies and cognate subjects. Also, it needs to be stressed that business schools as academic institutions have always faced a particular tension between the largely irreconcilable demands of being relevant to the world of business practice and possessing intellectual rigour and substance like other academic disciplines. Indeed, much of what goes on in a business school is an attempt to resolve this tension.

We have seen in Chapter 2, how from 1950s onwards, mainstream management has been engaged in imbibing the positivist methods of the sciences so as to produce supposedly valid, reliable knowledge on par with other established scientific disciplines. Seen in this light, CMS, despite its incessant critique of management scholarship, ironically end up adding reputational capital and academic respectability to the mainstream business school. Its deep theoretical anchorage in critical traditions of social scientific knowledge provides much needed academic rigour to an otherwise insufficiently 'rigorous' area of scholarship – the mainstream management. At present, it would incur reputational damage to business schools if the latter try doing away with all CMS academics they are institutional homes to.

Conversely, as some observers have noted, CMS has emerged as a fertile ground for the left-wing radical intellectuals to gain status and influence in the business school despite their ideological incompatibility. In any case, CMS remains a work-in-progress. It has managed to produce a loose oppositional identity by its consistent negation of the political and epistemological premises of mainstream management. But, even now, it is very difficult to surmise as to what CMS stands for. Various scholars, at different points of time, have attempted to give us a sense of the shared ethos of the CMS. For instance, Alvesson and Willmott (1992a) wanted to establish 'emancipation' as the key motif of Critical Management Studies (1992). Other scholars have referred to other sets of 'epistemic virtues' (Daston and Galison 2007). For some, the impetus for scholarly engagement in the field comes from Foucault's notion of the critical attitude and fearless speech while others draw on Derrida's understanding of responsibility and undecidability (Grey 2002). Others remain wedded to the old styles of industrial relations and industrial sociology where they continue to privilege the classical theoretical resources of Max Weber. Still, others find it difficult to forget Karl Marx and Marx-inspired LPT of Henry Braverman to take wholeheartedly to the post-modernist discursivity of CMS. For such scholars, the emergence of the affluent worker, occupational community studies, the embourgeoisement thesis, the question of dignified work and the related intellectual ground prepared by Braverman's book *Labour and Monopoly Capital* (1974) is too engaging a scholarly field to get submerged by the identity and subjectivity issues of certain streams of CMS.

For sociologists contributing to a journal like *Work, Employment and Society* (since 1987), and going for an academically productive alliance with industrial relations academics, feminists and the sociologists of work, employment and organisations, is intellectually and institutionally no less satisfying than CMS. These scholars take umbrage at CMS's endeavour to reduce the broad complex of work, industry and employment to 'organising' that most of CMS academics have blindly followed. If one goes by the quantum of scholarly publications – journals, handbooks, readers, conference papers and the like – CMS has certainly arrived as a noteworthy critique of management education and studies. Besides publications, by virtue of their sheer institutional location in business schools, there is bound to be a certain degree of engagement between the mainstream and CMS in terms of teaching as well. It is not that the CMS academics are the most influential group of the institutions of management, but their presence can longer be totally ignored. The institutional gravitas of CMS has consistently grown, and that too from within them.

CMS is no longer seen as an import from outside (universities and social science disciplines) that has made home in the unfamiliar and inhospitable terrain of management education. Even though CMS's academic networks remain restricted and vary enormously across institutions and geographies, its development of a division within the American Academy of Management has surely raised its global profile. Slowly, but consistently, its influence is growing in North America in addition to its relatively greater visibility in countries such as United Kingdom, Sweden, Denmark, Norway, Australia, and New Zealand. The AOM conferences, the CMS-identified journals, the CMS conferences, and the cumulative transnational networks spawned by them have facilitated the fledgling CMS presence in countries like India as well. This is not to say that CMS forms part of each and every institution of management in all the countries where management education is on the offer. Even where it exists, it is more visible in areas like organization studies and the related subjects.

However, what ultimately matters is not only its existence, but also its growing presence across the board. In an interesting way, CMS academics have started contributing to the evaluations and rankings of business schools. As these evaluations are anchored in the academic parameters of the published research (than practice-oriented management training), the presence of CMS academics in business schools turns out to be the latter's advantage. The latter can frequently draw upon the former's quantum and quality of academic publications to further their reputational ranking in conventional scholarly terms (Grey 2007: 467).

All said and done, CMS does adhere to the well-established academic protocols of knowledge production and dissemination even when it puts forward its own agenda of 'critique'. In this sense, institutions of management have come to depend on (in an ironical fashion) CMS to further their own agenda of 'excellence' and to meet the increasing demands of academic governance and international accreditation (Butler and Spoelstra 2014: 538–50). In other words, CMS has come to act as a source of legitimacy for business schools as long as the latter looks at themselves as academic institutions on par with universities, and the management studies harbours the academic aspiration of being recognised as a serious scientific scholarly discipline.

Thus, CMS and the institutions of management appear to be in some kind of symbiotic relationship notwithstanding the grand rhetoric of their being fundamentally opposed to each other. The very presence of CMS in business schools reveals the latter's open and plural character. It demonstrates that the business schools are not out-and-out ideological actors constituting a 'cultural circuit of capitalism' (Thrift 2005) otherwise they would not have tolerated, if not encouraged, CMS under their roof. At the same time, CMS, though part of the business schools, retains moral ground without appearing as 'tainted' or 'compromised' as long as it retains its right to criticise business schools as instruments of global capitalism.

Viewed thus, CMS can be seen as a kind of perpetual 'ginger group' already somewhat incorporated in the institutional landscape of management education. As discussed in the foregoing chapters, institutions of management have often been pitted against universities in relation to their scholarly practices. On the one hand, institutions of management have to earn their legitimacy by being relevant and application-oriented to the world of business practice, on the other hand, they are supposed to be adequately academic like university departments. This duality of expectations has been the source of a perpetual tension for professional institutions of management. Not only have they been routinely criticised for their failures to meet the expectations of the business world but have also been chastised for their lack of academic rigour and intellectual substance. Indeed, much of what constitutes the mainstream of management education and research today has been a response to this tension. As mentioned earlier, the mainstream management studies' attempt to embrace the positivist methods of the sciences so as to produce, like other established academic disciplines, theoretical knowledge has been a strategy to browbeat its disciplinary critics. More than half a century later, CMS came onto the scene as a critique of this mainstream which had by then almost successfully negotiated the popular binary of 'rigour' and 'relevance'. Within this context, CMS, which began its journey as the fundamental critique of mainstream business school, has in course of time transformed into an avenue to earn academic respectability and scholarly reputation.

CMS and its limits: critique of a critique

CMS too has been subject to numerous critiques coming from all quarters, including from within CMS. Some observers have pointed out huge gap between the lofty ideals professed by CMS and its actual scholarly and institutional practices. Commentators have argued that CMS seldom lives up to its higher aims. While some take CMS scholars to task for not engaging with activists and other stakeholders outside the academy (Parker 2002), others point out that research produced under the auspices of CMS often lacks wider social and political relevance (Thompson 2004). At best, there is said to be a certain lack of consistency between word and deed among the CMS academics.

Though CMS scholars keep trumpeting about their epistemic virtues as compared to the mainstream management studies, they fail to acknowledge the changes in the latter. For example, there was a time when qualitative research and interpretivist methodology were the short end of the stick for the orthodox management research, which is no longer the case (Zald 2002). While most critical scholars offer paeans to non-positivist research, they overlook or simply ignore the appreciable changes (by their own parameters) in the practices of mainstream scholarship. More often than not, CMS academics have differing understandings of what *being critical* means in relation to their institutional location and, that is why, an emergent field like CMS has generated voluminous literature that is highly polemical in nature with hair-splitting arguments about differing nuances of the term 'critical' (Spicer, Alvesson and Kärreman 2009; Butler and Spoelstra 2014: 538–50). That is why, CMS exists as a broad open intellectual tent where anyone with the self-image of being a critical scholar can be found amidst an overall chaotic theoretical milieu (Parker 2010). CMS does have the zeal of a social movement in terms of distinguishing insignia of conferences, journals and the like, but lacks a unifying platform for constructive intervention. After all, the CMS academics believe that a critical scholar has no obligation to come up with an alternative plan of action. Critique, whatever it means, is an overwhelming political and intellectual act that obviates the need for other co-ordinates of programmatic action.

Commentators have frequently referred to the tenuous position held by CMS academics in management institutions. Since the revolutionary Marxist message is avowedly anti-managerial and anti-capitalist, there is no surprise if business schools did not have a major presence of left scholars. However, as mentioned earlier, the LPT attracted the attention of a group of Marxist scholars in business schools during the 1980s (Rowlinson and Hassard 2000: 85–111). Even otherwise, after the historical defeat of the left since its heyday of 1968, the revolutionary destiny of the proletariat underwent a change of conceptualisation. The degradation of labour in capitalist work organisations started getting seen in relation to the cultural characteristics of global capitalism under the influence of Hegelian Frankfurt School presided over by theorists such as Adorno, Marcuse, Horkheimer, and Habermas.[2] The earlier type of Marxian eschatology gave way to notions of repressive tolerance, one-dimensional man and mass society. The French philosopher Michel Foucault emerged as the most influential presiding deity of discursive radicalism. Discourse became the new mantra of radical politics calibrated for the neo-liberal times.

Other theoretical tendencies contributed their might to the newly instituted grand questioning of history, progress, science and reason.[3] Fragments acquired celebratory status, relativism and deconstruction became ends in themselves. The older types of studies of the dynamics of work organisations within capitalist corporations became less fashionable. The investment of intellectual energy went for a thoroughgoing critique of managerialism *tout court*. Subjectivity and identity turned out be new conceptual pegs to hang one's political and ideological stance. Through all these changes, CMS ended up monopolising the term 'critical' in a way that it alienated large number of sociologists of work, employment and organisations, who all were dubbed as the apologists of the orthodox management studies.

Arguably, the rise of CMS did expand the intellectual frontiers of the critical theory by forging new intersections with the field of management scholarship. However, the ascent of CMS also meant recasting sociology and other foundational disciplines in a manner that suited its ideological agenda. The work done by the hitherto existing social science constituencies within business schools was made to appear complicit with the hidden political agenda of global capitalism. This amounted to downplaying the robust empirical and theoretical work done by the scores of sociologists of work and employment and organisations since the days of classical sociology. After all, the capitalist employment relationship, the bureaucratic organisation and the division of labour were central concepts for the classical sociologists. Much of meaningful sociological work that contributed to the development of sociology in Europe and North America concerned itself with intersections of class and work (Parker 2013: 170–1).

As a matter of fact, the rise of CMS coincided with the rise of culturalism within sociology and the growing popularity of the cultural studies in general. The grand theorists of late modernity and postmodernity started contesting the primacy of work as the pivot of one's identity. Ideas about production and the shop floor seemed to be giving way to an image of consumers operating in a society of shopping malls, symbols, simulacra, and hyper-reality. Employment was no longer being seen as the central (or only) category to understand total social organisation of labour. The newly emerged fields of sociologies of gender, youth, and ethnicity brought out the limitations of the earlier research on work (Elger 2009; Beynon 2011; Besio, du Gay and Velarde 2020).

In the United Kingdom especially, the realisation soon dawned that much of sociology of work was essentially studies of white men in factory. Surely, this type of work not only looked rather old-fashioned but was also impervious to the other fault lines of identity like race, gender, and ethnicity (Abreu-Pederzini and Suarez-Barraza 2019). As a consequence, in the wake of CMS, a stark opposition started emerging between those studying work and employment and those studying organisations. The former invited the indifference and (even a certain disdain) for their type of conventional social scientific empirical work. All of them were painted with the broad brush as positivists for their archaic protocols for the selection, presentation and analysis of data. These positivists (sociologists of the old school) became the undesirable end of the binary to be consistently and persistently opposed with such novel theoretical and methodological resources as identity, discourse, narrative, culture. Terms which had acquired the stability of a noun in earlier research were loosened up and rendered a verb all over again. Thus, organisations were rethought as the acts of organising; conceptual categories of gender, class, occupation appeared complicit in the making of oppressive meta-narratives and the quest for alternatives became an end in itself (Vijay and Varman 2017).

CMS became the harbinger of the incessant problematisation of key themes like corporate organisation, the ideology of managerialism, the managerial class or capitalism per se. It triumphantly privileged the theoretical as the site for critical work. In its reading, it was not necessarily the structures of the world which were the springboard for concern, but structures of thought – the habitual, the common sense, and the taken for granted (Parker 2013: 172). One can easily contrast this preoccupation with discourse and narrative that CMS has fostered with earlier social anthropological understanding where someone like Radcliff-Brown would see social structure as a tangible entity as a seashell. CMS academics, instead, privileged new imaginings of the social, and called for new methods, and new sites for investigation. Their sociological orientations were conditioned by the extant theories of globalisation underlining space-time compression, global distribution of production, the changed context of flexible working and the intersectionality of multiple bases of identity in the labour market.

Even those students who had been trained in sociology along the lines of sociology being a critical humanist discipline with the debunking motif being its core (Nisbet 1976; Berger 1992) found the new-found critical enthusiasm of CMS academics as the typically overstated case of new zealots arraigned again the older world of scholarship. Anything and everything that had something to do with relevant useful knowledge for management came under the critical scrutiny of CMS. For the latter, everyone except those adhering to CMS, were the prisoners of lucre of money, privilege and better chances of career mobility that management institutions provided for. CMS academics had almost exclusive access to the power of critique whereas others were mere careerists given to the conservative political ethos of the business schools.

Against these people who had been selling the positivist idea of a social science based on values of truth, value neutrality, and valid knowledge, CMS brought in its weapon in the form of a contingent politics of representation challenging the earlier epistemological certitude of the social scientific practices that were widely prevalent in the academy including institutions of management. It started with the cultivated self-image of a novel epistemological challenge to the very possibility of a social science in a value neutral manner. For CMS, the political became an infinitely expansive and elastic term. On this count, everything becomes political: the way one thinks (or does not think) and writes (or does not write). Knowledge was always power. Everything needed to be reimagined and thought afresh. The earlier politics of truth and knowledge needed to be thoroughly interrogated to unleash alternative faculties of imagination (Mignolo 2000, 2007).

However, some observers have charged 'critters' (a US term for CMS academics) to be a group of disaffected academic drifters with an overblown sense of their radicalism. They argue that critters' self-imposed estrangement from the mainstream management scholarship ends up as system-supportive critique of the traditional management studies

(TMS). It was never meant to replace it. Rather, its aim has been to open up a critical field of management studies in the institutional and scholarly interstices of the TMS. The very legitimacy of the field of CMS (criticalmanagement.org) depends on the continued dominance of the TMS against which the CMS established itself since approximately the mid-1990s.

It is customary to underline that Alvesson and Willmott (1992a) chose to publish their version of the inaugural manifesto of the CMS, "On the Idea of Emancipation in Management" in the *Academy of Management Review*, the epitome of mainstream scholarship in management. This, in a way, indicates that the CMS is part of management standard's canon (Klikauer 2011, 2015a, 2015b, 2015c). Since then, according to Klikauer (2018), CMS has set itself up as a management-sustaining critical feedback loop in support of the TMS. While CMS does not have a single mouthpiece by way of a journal, there are journals in the field which are known as the CMS journals: *International Journal of Production Economics, Journal of Business Ethics, British Journal of Management (BJM), European Journal of Operational Research, Journal of Management Studies (JMS), Human Relations, Organization Studies Organization, Management Learning, Administrative Science Quarterly, Critical Perspectives on International Business*, etc. (Klikauer 2018: 756).

CMS has been charged to be living by offering a system-corrective and system-stabilising critique to the TMS. It prefers to present itself to TMS as an enlightened force that is able to identify some of the shortcomings of TMS in order to improve the latter. Some of these commentators also question the origin myths that CMS has given to themselves: that it originated, at least in parts, in the Frankfurt School of critical theory. But what the CMS scholars actually write is quite distant from the spirit of the Frankfurt School of critical theory (Klikauer 2015b). Whereas critical theory's telos is universal emancipation, 'the attempt by a group or a class to emancipate themselves from particular oppressive social conditions' (Klikauer 2018: 755), 'CMS telos is micro-emancipation, the production of better managers, good management, [the] shap[ing of] organisations to become fairer, and the idea that management's social engineering can be balanced' (Klikauer 2015c: 207).

CMS's monumental effort to anchor itself in the hermeneutical and interpretive methodological traditions and its celebration of 'reflexivity' though have hardly shielded it from the charge of being an academic club of largely white men and some women. Its persistent invocation of diversity is yet to be translated into the socially diverse base of its practitioners in terms of gender, race, ethnicity, and nationality (Tatli 2012). It remains steeped in the epistemological dominance of Western knowledge systems with only lip service to the epistemologies of the South (Santos 2014). Their invocation of 'southern theory' is in effect a tribute to the post-colonial studies emanating out of the North American campuses with the increasing presence of Diaspora scholars. Of course, it has brought out in the open the ideological biases and shortcomings of the mainstream discourse of management practice and theory. It has underlined the need to reflect upon the role of critical pedagogy in management education and the attendant roles of the business schools, something that has been absent from the general academic analysis. It has accorded a centrality to politics to self-reflexively think about organizations and work relations in relation to power and domination. It has attempted to probe the rules, routines, and organizational practices to retrieve the disorder, uncertainty, and insecurity that lurk beneath the surface.

But then, as Zald (2002) asks, in his rather sympathetic review of CMS, is it fated to be a marginal enterprise in the context of the institutions of management, or is it going to acquire centrality? Are CMS academics perpetual mavericks always exhibiting contrarian tendencies against the dominant ethos of the institutions they work for? Or, are they condemned to some kind of schizoid existence where they remain deeply critical of institutions and constituencies that provide them with bread and butter? Indeed, there cannot be definitive answers to these questions. The field of management education, despite all the efforts made so far, is far from being a homogeneous field. There are different models of management and different sets of assumptions that inform the theory and practice of management. If management is seen in the mode of engineering/problem solving, then, evidently, CMS will have less scope to expand and flourish. On the contrary, if it is seen in the mode of enlightenment knowledge, then CMS has the room to bring in critical reflexive methodologies. Also, the different domains of management make a difference so far as receptivity to CMS is concerned. As Zald (2002: 380) mentions, CMS may have more to say on issues like worker–management relations, the role and responsibility of the corporation and business towards society, and sustainability. If the ultimate touchstone of management gets defined in terms of the bottom line, CMS may not have much to offer.

Be that as it may, CMS has acquired an independent identity within the institutional context of management education and research thanks to the concerted efforts of its flag-bearers whose intellectual energy and commitment helped build it over the past quarter of a century. Nevertheless, viewed from a distance, CMS appears to be a 'critical-theoretical' island amidst the everyday uncriticality of the mainstream management. Paradoxically though, CMS 'requires the mainstream both intellectually, as its other, and institutionally, as its paymaster' (Grey 2007: 463–71). One may surmise that CMS draws its intellectual and institutional sustenance from the very existence of the mainstream studies whose practices it finds fundamentally flawed. It remains a moot point if CMS imparts legitimation to the mainstream, or it is the other way round. Moreover, CMS's critique of the mainstream presupposes an implausible homogeneity of the latter. It discounts the possibility of the mainstream being as varied as itself. Also, it undermines the value and significance of the earlier critical work on management that preceded the CMS label (Klikauer 2018).

While it is true that CMS foregrounded the necessity of critique and managed to expand the scope of critical work with a renewed sense of widespread legitimacy, it fused the act of critique with its own label (Grey 2007: 463–71). In any case, as Parker (2013: 167) avers, 'CMS shouts loudly about emancipation, but is cloistered in well-paid jobs in shiny new business schools'. For many of its critics, CMS doesn't seem to have achieved any discernible impact on the practices of the mainstream world of management education save its vague set of critical platitudes and political grandstanding. At least for most industrial sociologists or industrial relations academics of the earlier generation, CMS was a motley group of 'radical' intellectuals piggy-riding the social sciences' fashionable turn to culture, language, discourse, narrative, and critical theory. For the Marxists too, CMS was a form of intellectual indulgence leading to the side-tracking of the concrete problems of the world: capitalist forms of economic organization, patriarchal structures of power, global imperialism. Even today there is no agreement on what the word 'critical' means, thereby facilitating the big-tent approach of accommodating a variety of perspectives: as an umbrella research orientation CMS embraces various theoretical traditions including Critical Theory, Marxism, post-Marxism, post-structuralism, post-modernism, feminism, post-colonialism, psychoanalysis, and ecology representing a pluralistic, multi-disciplinary movement.[4] Likewise, its website[5] presents the following list of illustrative topics:

- critical theories of the nature of managerial authority, resistance to managerial authority, identity, affectivity, rationality, and subjectivity;
- critiques of managerialist theories of management and organization;
- critical assessments of emerging alternative forms of organization;

- critiques of political economy;
- critical perspectives on business strategy, globalization, entrepreneurship, technological innovation, and computerization;
- critical analyses of discourses of management, development, and progress;
- critical perspectives on class, gender, and race; the profit-imperative and the natural environment;
- critical epistemologies and methodologies.

There seem to be no topics that cannot be prefaced with the word 'critical', no limits on what critical work could be applied to.

CMS's 'goals and objectives' are stated as follows:

The overall goal of our research, teaching, and extra-curricular activities is to contribute to the creation of better organizations, more humane societies, and a viable world system. Our specific objectives within the Academy of Management are to serve existing members' needs well so that growth in the Interest Group occurs, to generate high-quality dialogue in our meetings, to encourage the diffusion of our ideas and values in research and teaching, and to build bridges to progressive social movements to contribute to positive change for social and environmental welfare.

This is fine rhetoric, but who is to determine the meaning of words like 'better', 'humane', 'progressive', and 'positive'? It is easy to invoke theoretical terms like 'capitalism', 'neo-liberalism', 'patriarchy' but difficult to escape from their effects in personal and professional lives. And ultimately, CMS remains a creature of the Global North, which is not an enabling and impressive basis on which to claim CMS's grandiloquent goals and objectives. It would be presumptuous to claim that CMS represents a diverse range of people and interests (Tatli 2012).

Conclusion: the shifting trajectories of CMS

Over the quarter of a century, CMS as an 'evolving body of knowledge' (Alvesson, Bridgman and Willmott 2009: 1) has turned out to be an umbrella intellectual marker for a range of scholarly practices being undertaken by academics adhering to multiple research traditions and acts of theorizing. While its core task of transforming the conventional management studies remains its prime driving force, its internal dynamics have led to a wobbly heterogeneity to an extent where its very concerns appear to meander in different directions – from old-school Marxism to various streams of post-modern and post-structuralist pontifications on knowledge, power, and representation.

While this diversity chimes well with the relativistic stances of many of its protagonists, it runs the danger of not being impactful enough to make a serious dent in the institutionalised practices of the conventional management studies more generally. Its consistent and prolonged agonizing over-reflexive scholarly practices make it susceptible to not being taken seriously by mainstream management researchers. Notwithstanding its discreteness as a critical movement in the context of institutions of management, it remains too broad and too fragmented to have a unifying voice. No wonder CMS has witnessed periodic attempts by its proponents and sympathisers to put forth its key characteristics to lend it a coherence and unification which it obviously lacks (Fournier and Grey 2000; Adler, Paul du Gay and Reed 2014; Delbridge, 2014). Time and again, we are reminded of a number of key themes that are common to work in the field of CMS: the questioning of the taken-for-granted, moving beyond instrumentalism and assumptions of performativity, the concern for reflexivity and meanings in research, and the challenging of structures of domination.

These reiterations have somehow allowed CMS to monopolise the entire tradition of critique that had origins in social sciences before its advent. It is as if CMS invented the critical appraisal of management for the first time and nothing critical existed prior to its emergence. Yet, it has been marked with bitter and protracted debates about its own boundaries and identities: some want it to be open and accommodative, whereas others tend to argue for making it restrictive to impart it a distinctive, coherent, and recognisable identity. Some 'lean in the direction of a view of CMS that is accommodating rather than restrictive whilst, at the same time, being mindful of the danger of being so open-minded and liberal that it includes everything and so ends up being a vacuous category' (Alvesson et al. 2009: 7).

At the end of the day, CMS is identified by the set of substantive themes that its practitioners take up for research and their self-identification as CMS scholars. Also, there is no denying that CMS has posed fundamental challenges (howsoever unsuccessfully) to the basic assumptions, conventions, and the dominant norms of mainstream professional management studies. It has tried to disrupt the comfort zone of professional management research and practice through reminders that the apparently self-contained world of business management is embedded in the larger historical, political, and economic contexts. Apart from other features discussed in the foregoing, it is CMS's challenge to the existing status quo that has given it a sharp critical edge. Some, if not most, of the CMS academics have an explicit goal of radically transforming contemporary management practices and organizational systems. A politicized agenda of change is a central motif of CMS, which places it in sharp distinction with much mainstream management theory. It is this problematization of the (increasingly homogenous) norms and conventions in management theorizing and research that should be seen as central to the CMS's contribution to management studies (Delbridge 2014).

However, the very nature of the enterprise of CMS gives rise to a number of questions pertaining to its overall objectives and actual accomplishments. Given its location amidst institutions of management, there are usual questions about the very possibility of a radical management science. Some observers find CMS a contradiction in terms, some sort of oxymoron. Indeed, CMS lacks an unequivocal definition. But that does not negate its ascendance as a broad movement with some key shared themes and concerns. It is on the basis of a shared understanding of its key attributes that CMS has become increasingly institutionalized within the discipline of management studies (Zald 2002). As mentioned earlier, there are now large dedicated international conferences, workshops, journals, doctoral programmes, and handbooks that go under the rubric of CMS besides the CMS scholars' interventions in general management journals proposing radical critique of, and possible alternatives to, the conventional management studies.

As a matter of fact, CMS has raised more questions than it has provided answers for. It has taken upon itself the mandate of making business schools more critical. Noticeably though, the critical reflexive gaze of CMS fails to fall upon the mechanisms of hierarchy and exclusion that operate within its own community of practitioners. Like any other oppositional movement, it has developed its own orthodoxies in the course of time with the tendency to close ranks for those with perspectives different from theirs. Besides its lack of demographic diversity and excesses of verbalism, it remains indifferent to its own embeddedness in and relations of power and hegemony and its role in sustaining and reproducing these structures in their own institutions and communities. This is in sharp contrast to CMS's task of offering a transformatory agenda to promote emancipation from the relations of power and inequality through a critique of mainstream management practice and scholarship (Alvesson and Willmott 1992a). Moreover, CMS scholars themselves are not immune to the rules, codes, and habits of the academic field. They end up following the same pathways of 'excellence' that the mainstream framework of academic careerism dictates. They are hardly the academic renouncers who have completely given up on their career concerns, notwithstanding their righteousness. The binary of the mainstream and the critical in terms of management allows CMS to be oblivious of its own closure to other critical traditions. It is rather quick to dub anything that does not adhere to its philosophical positions as uncritical besides drawing an overblown distinction between CMS and the 'mainstream'.

Tatli (2012) is unsparing in his attack on CMS for it replicates the wide-ranging symbolic violence in academia by keeping silent about the exclusionary mechanisms that keep CMS community homogeneous in terms of not only theoretical approaches but also the demographic make-up of its members. Adler et al. (2014: 925) is concerned that CMS may become 'a closed community of like-minded people'. According to Clegg et al. (2006: 11) this has already happened: 'CMS research is a relatively closed system that does not interact empathetically with others – it preaches to the converted and damns the heathen others'. The parochial nature of CMS research and community has been criticised by a growing number of scholars (Parker 2014; Klikauer 2018). For Tatli (2012), in many instances, the mainstream may be more receptive than CMS of critical work that does not subscribe to the 'desired' approach.

This paradigmatic closure is compounded by the demographic homogeneity of mostly white, heterosexual, western, able-bodied men acting as Division Chairs in the Academy of Management, thereby making CMS a closed and non-diverse community. This goes against the constitutive logic of CMS, whose political objective is to challenge hegemonic relations of power and authority and to speak for the silenced and the oppressed (Grey 2002). Arguably, the very exclusivity of CMS goes against its espoused moral and political commitment to tackling injustice, discrimination, hegemony and inequality. For instance, Parker (1995: 560) says that the role of critical management scholars is to point to the 'reproduction of inequalities of gender, sexuality, ethnicity, disability, age and socio-economic class'. In the Academy of Management domain statement CMS Interest Group is described as follows:

> *Our premise is that structural features of contemporary society, such as the profit imperative, patriarchy, racial inequality, and ecological irresponsibility often turn organizations into instruments of domination and exploitation. Driven by a shared desire to change this situation, we aim in our research, teaching, and practice to develop critical interpretations of management and society and to generate radical alternatives.*

Tatli (2012) rightfully asks: How can a community which is characterized by the numerical and hierarchical domination of the privileged segments of society provide alternatives for the disadvantaged and oppressed? And why does it believe that it has a right to do so anyway? For him, 'the problem lies in the fact that although CMS has a sharp eye in spotting the workings of exclusion and privilege outside, it conveniently turns a blind eye to the underrepresentation of women, racial and ethnic minorities, non-western scholars in the CMS ranks'. ... 'Consequently, the narrow demographic make-up of CMS is rarely mentioned and, when it is mentioned, it is explained by the non-diverse make-up of the management academy in general'. After all, [the] 'claims of being political and emancipatory come with an added "burden" of the responsibility to challenge exclusion and inequality not only outside but also within'.

CMS becomes nothing more than just another area in management studies where individuals who have access to 'right' discourses know the 'right' people and own the social and cultural capitals that are considered legitimate by the CMS community become influential. Then, how marginal is the marginal with its own pecking orders and ring-fencing mechanisms (Tatli 2012)? Although the CMS Academy of Management domain statement is encompassing enough to accommodate different approaches as long as they have a critical intent in exploring organizations, in reality, CMS has been institutionalized as a representative of post-modern and post-structuralist approaches to organizational research. This theoretical closure alienates critical researchers who commit themselves to ontologies and theoretical perspectives that CMS is not subscribed to. Furthermore, with its hard-to-understand lexicon CMS forecloses any possibilities of this body of knowledge being understood and used by practitioners or academics who are outside the CMS circle. What is the use of 'critical' and 'emancipatory' theory that does not seem to care to communicate its message to the others? CMS researchers need to engage in debates with their 'mainstream' others and produce relevant and actionable knowledge, instead of remaining satisfied with 'the self- referential, self-citing discursive debates that are carried out in a small and tightly knit community'. If CMS scholars 'turn a blind eye to the mechanisms of oppression, exclusion, and toxic networks that are sustained within CMS despite their commitment to justice and fairness in organizations and in society at large, they will become the preachers of principles that they do not apply to themselves' (Tatli 2012: 26).

CMS critiques the philosophical and political basis of management. It is not about the amelioration of unethical, undignified, and inhuman workplace practices that necessarily accompany the onwards march of global capitalism. It counters the ideological missions of business schools by talking about its not-so-beautiful underbelly. To be sure, CMS presupposes and entails a degree of courage on the part of its proponents who undertake their critical work within the boundaries of mainstream institutions of management. It is like 'a trade unionist trying to build membership where it is forbidden' (Grey 2002: 506).

However, in the course of time, CMS has also acquired ameliorative tendencies to make itself ideologically acceptable and institutionally palatable (Alvesson et al. 2009). In the process, it has attracted the charge of being diluted and compromised (Klikauer 2018). Yet, for some, CMS continues to remain an intellectual ghetto walling itself off from everything it designates as orthodox or conventional or mainstream approach to management.

While CMS may take decades to convert the mainstream to its critical approach, its continuous questioning of the mainstream, and its positioning as a politically viable alternative to the mainstream orthodoxy, is worthy of acknowledgement and appreciation. At all events, it does have a following, and with the passage of time, academic legitimacy and institutional recognition as well. As a consequence, today the onus is on the business schools to keep reflecting on its purpose beyond its contributions to the economic and technical efficiency of the capitalist firm. An institution of management can no longer afford to be a finishing school ostensibly socializing managers into business etiquettes and legitimating management as a socially prestigious occupation and profession. Part of the credit must go to CMS if management journals today carry discussions of gender, ethnicity, power, the environment, sustainability, social responsibility, and the like. CMS has surely pushed the envelope: management education, of necessity, defends itself in terms that go beyond their hitherto primary concerns of status and legitimation, profit and productivity, the bottom-line, and the balance sheet. If nothing else, CMS is a constant reminder of the possibility of the opening up of the world of management education and scholarship to new challenges emanating from the ever-evolving and ever-shifting fault lines of the increasingly complex human world of classes, countries, ideologies, identities, and subjectivities. Yet, its 'uncritical' reliance on critical social theory has appeared to have rendered it into an obsessively self-occupied and self-mutating oppositional academic-intellectual discourse undermining both sociology and a robust tradition of empirical social research that has equally, if not predominantly, been part of sociology's enduring legacy.

Notes

1. The term 'cow sociology' is attributed to Daniel Bell (1956: 25). The basic idea being the more satisfied the worker is, the greater his self-esteem will be, the more contented he will be, and therefore, the more efficient in what he is doing (Parker 2013: 178).
2. For an intelligible summary of the theorists of the Frankfurt School and its critics, see Bottomore (2002).
3. Michel Foucault's work has generated a voluminous literature in the humanities and social sciences. For a concise introduction to his palpable academic impact see Llyod and Thacker (1997).
4. http://criticalmanagement.org accessed on 28 August 2020.
5. https://cms.aom.org/ accessed on 28 August 2020.

5 Conclusion
Disciplinarity, inter-disciplinarity, and the new academy

The prism of disciplinarity-inter-disciplinarity provides a useful way of looking at the history of modern academy and its institutional structure. This serves as a useful, meaningful perspective to make sense of the historically evolving interaction between sociology and management education. Most academic disciplines have a tendency to invoke an imaginary golden age from their disciplinary past when confronted with the challenge of inter-disciplinarity. Concomitantly, they have a primal fear of getting lost into disciplinary indistinctiveness if exposed to the overwhelming sway of an inter-disciplinary field. This probably explains why even a field of knowledge that began its journey as an inter-disciplinary field goes out of the way to acquire the insignia and identity of a distinctive discipline. Nothing illustrates this better than the case of management studies and, to an extent, sociology as well. Academic disciplines work under the burden of maintaining a coherent and unified theoretical, methodological and substantive identity lest the gravitational pull of their disciplinary core gets weakened and/or leads to the successful establishment of their various subject-areas into separate sub-disciplines or studies. Sociology as an academic discipline has been perennially ridden by this anxiety of disciplinary fission to the extent of acknowledging its impossibility as a bounded discipline.

Likewise, as the preceding chapters have discussed, most academic disciplines (save humanities) aspire for a scientific status to gain in scholarly esteem and public approbation. Sociology has been unequivocal in its pursuit of establishing itself as the proper science of the social in the same way as management has been preoccupied with vociferously establishing its claims of being a science of business operations and organisations. The competing disciplinary claims get shifted to the domains of substantive themes (the subject matter) and explanatory prowess. Disciplines with greater theoretical sophistication, methodological acuity, and clarity of the

DOI: 10.4324/9781003257813-5

substantive arena win over others in occupying higher echelons of the system of disciplinary stratification. Disciplines like sociology with an irredeemably contradictory core and a fractal make-up keep struggling to lay claim to its disciplinary distinctiveness. Its defining identity as the study of the 'social' gets disarrayed as the latter neither lends itself to an unproblematic repertoire of explanatory concepts for sociologists nor to something that can be established as the ground of critique (Abbott 2001: 14). In other words, the disciplinary system obtaining in the modern academy is never a settled terrain. Despite its apparent stability, it remains continually exposed to forces of change.

In any case, a generalist discipline like sociology stands to lose in competition with other specialised, well-demarcated ones. At a time when the inter-disciplinary study and research is frequently invoked as the new norm of academic governance, different disciplines are likely to incur uneven and varying kinds of gains/losses. Some disciplines are likely to expand their disciplinary influence under inter-disciplinary regime, whereas others might fear their shrinkage and further loss of influence. Evidently, the consequences of inter-disciplinarity have not been even across disciplines. That is why some disciplines are ever willing to cede to inter-disciplinary areas, and yet, others hesitate, if not outrightly reject, to join the inter-disciplinary bandwagon.

As disciplines, both sociology and management have the shared fortune of not having the highest degree of distinctiveness in 'theory, method and substance' notwithstanding their systematic character and institutionally recognised disciplinary identity. They are relatively deficient as the repository of abstract, problem-portable knowledge. Their degrees of abstraction are under-developed when compared to a discipline like economics. Both are 'polycentric' disciplines with porous boundaries and weak boundary-maintaining mechanisms. They work under the constant pressure of producing problem-based applied knowledge. At the same time, they are expected to be sufficiently abstract through their concepts and methods to acquire scholarly heights. In a sense, both appear to be saddled with the 'residual' problems of other disciplines owing to their disciplinary origins. In both cases, their methodological and conceptual claims have so far not managed the requisite epistemological break to be designated as the proper forms of science. They have raging internal debates on their status as disciplines belonging to social sciences and humanities. They relatively fare poorly in comparison to the ordered nature of other disciplines. Both are informed by an eclecticism that is seen as problematic in terms of their internal organization.

Both the disciplines exist in a perennial state of inter-disciplinarity. The latter shapes their internal order and external relations to other disciplines. This inter-disciplinarity makes them susceptible to fractal splitting when sub-areas of the discipline migrate to constitute new subject fields or become part of applied subject areas. This frequently leads to a shift in self-identification on part of the practitioners making parent disciplines fuzzier still. Thus, 'sociologists' become 'criminologists', 'social policy' analysts, and the like. And, management academics become experts in areas like marketing, strategy, international business, and the likes. These characteristics make their claims to methodological distinctiveness rather weak and untenable.[1] (For instance, sociology has no claim to any distinctive methodological tool, unlike psychology (with its experiments), anthropology (with ethnographic fieldwork), history (with its archives), and economics with its elegant theoretical models (Holmwood 2010: 645).

More importantly, both the disciplines are part of a global institutional complex shaped by external factors of the wider socio-political environment. This global institutional complex of higher education is undeniably dominated by the United States. Academics and scholars in much of the world work in the shadow of this central complex in terms of their disciplinary practices. They have to negotiate constantly what the Beninese philosopher Paulin Hountondji (1997) has called 'extroversion', that is, the stance required of intellectual workers in the global periphery to orient themselves to intellectual authority that comes from outside. They need to learn the concepts and methods that are taught at the Harvard Business School and the University of California. They need to travel to the countries in the global North to study or update their knowledge. They are expected to publish in global (read American) journals, to attend American conferences, and join American networks. In sociology at least, there has been an engaging debate on this centre-periphery relations in the context of knowledge production (Connell 2017; Connell et al. 2017). However, management as a discipline has been largely oblivious of its uncritical dependence on the metropolitan models and theoretical frameworks.

Encouragingly, the rise of the Critical Management Studies (CMS) has brought into focus some of these unstated assumptions. In some quarters, there is an attempt for professional independence from the hegemonic U.S. influence by way of seeking knowledge relevant to local societies, and the active cultivation of local traditions and audiences (Mignolo 2007; Santos 2014). Yet, the flow of theoretical frameworks and models remains uncomfortably one-sided: mainly from the Global North to the Global South. The sad truth is that an academic's

Conclusion 97

worldwide recognition largely follows from the acknowledgement and appreciation of her scholarly contributions in the United States. Even European theorists like Habermas, Foucault, Derrida, and Bourdieu acquired international influence in the wake of their endorsement in the American campuses. Once influential and significant centres of social sciences, like the *Ecole des Hautes Etudes en Sciences Sociales* in Paris and the London School of Economics and Political Science too, are increasingly under the American sway.

Noticeably, like other academic disciplines, sociology and management are embedded in an unequal global economy of knowledge production. The latter, of necessity, creates a hierarchy of academic institutions whereby the elite ones are from the Global North, the centre. This hierarchy entails a division of labour, in which the data flow into the centre from the peripheries: generally the centre arrogates the right to assemble and process data and export developed concepts and methods to the rest of the world (Connell 2017). As stated earlier, the CMS has spawned critical discussions about the asymmetries of the current socio-economic context and the need for alternative formulations of theoretical paradigms and knowledge claims.

The preceding chapters have repeatedly emphasized sociology's lack of a unitary or clearly bounded structure (Bernstein 2000; Urry 1995). It exemplifies a horizontal knowledge structure, 'meaning that it comprises a series of specialised codes or languages (corresponding to theoretical approaches) and that, unlike hierarchical knowledge structures, it lacks any integrating codes that could provide for the development of general theory' (Bernstein 2000: 161–3). Observers keep insisting on sociology's inherently inter-disciplinary structure (Cooper 2012: 83; Holmwood 2010). Whereas this trait makes it particularly vulnerable to the current 'mode 2' regime of governance where the emphasis is on inter-disciplinary applied studies, it also endows it as an engaging critical discipline. Not surprisingly, sociology has been the fountainhead of the CMS, even today, is an important source for critical responses to manifold transformations in academic governance. Of course, there is no denying that the senses in which sociology can be seen as critical are themselves related to its fractured existence as a discipline.

As a matter of fact, while sociology's claim as a critical discipline has wider appeal, including in institutions of management through the CMS, there is chaotic understanding of the key operative term – critical. By contrast, there is broader consensus that critique is the main purpose of the discipline. Of late, as Chapter 4 has discussed, there is growing criticism of the enterprise of critique and its ethical and epistemological arrogance. Be that as it may, sociology, as an academic discipline, remains indispensable to any critical endeavour for it speaks of matters that established powers and entrenched interests would prefer not to come out in the open: poverty, inequality, violence, exploitation, identity, subjecthood, justice, dignity, patriarchy, race, ethnicity, and imperialism of categories. It has historically acquired the skill of unpacking the underbelly of a phenomenon in all its meticulous details, and it can speak about them in not so flattering a manner. It has consistently stressed the need to historicise and unravel the taken-for-granted character of multiple forms of power, privilege, and interest constellations. Most importantly, it speaks the language of change and transformation. In a way, it can very well serve the functions of a discipline that unsettles and unnerves the powers-to-be. In its critical avatar, it can be a challenge, and an antidote, to the ruling ideology of the day. Given its continuing preoccupation with the collective, the community, and the social, it can very well present a notion of the public, or public interest, which can go against the very grain of reigning individualism and has the long-cultivated ability to offend the sensibilities of the powerful and the dominant, be they nations, communities, or social groups.

The debate about merits and demerits of inter-disciplinarity has become an inalienable part of contemporary forms of academic governance. There are multiple claims made for inter-disciplinarity in modern academy. The disciplinary status of sociology and management is necessarily connected with the persistent call for inter-disciplinarity. Even as there rests a plausible case against certain forms of advocacy of inter-disciplinarity, there is no escape from inter-disciplinary research and teaching, especially in an institution of management. Inter-disciplinary project is to stay for the time being, here and elsewhere. Disciplines like sociology and management cannot turn away from an engagement with the institutions wherein they are located and their spokespersons.

Such an engagement acquires added complexity in the context of higher education, where academics are deeply implicated in the making and unfolding of neoliberal governance. The forms of institutional governance become an inescapable part of an academic's life and impinge on her disciplinary practices. The norms of academic governance are as much part of the texture of academic life as the disciplinary ethos. There is need for critical vigilance on the part of contemporary academics about both the demands of academic-institutional governance and the intellectual claims of the disciplines that they belong to. Undoubtedly, nothing is self-evident, neither the disciplinary claims to truth nor the inter-disciplinary zing about innovation and flexibility. Simultaneously, criticality is not a pre-given disciplinary virtue. It needs continuous re-working and continual refinement in relation to context and contemporaneity. It is important to remember that academics and scholars are embedded in the same systems of governance about which they make critical judgment. In what follows, we pick out certain connecting threads between sociology and management education in India, which may potentially turn out to be mutually beneficial and enriching in academic and institutional terms.

In Chapter 3, we have seen how the limited engagement between sociology and management education has been a function of two interrelated factors: the peculiar history of Indian sociology and the growing urge of management studies to develop as a distinctive discipline by reducing its reliance on foundational social sciences. So far as the first aspect is concerned, it is important to remember that sociologists in India did not accord requisite scholarly attention to economic processes and phenomena for a variety of reasons. This evidently limited sociology's repertoire of empirical work and conceptual and theoretical resources to contribute to management studies, for the latter essentially focuses on economic side of our collective life. This need not have been the case as India offers a particularly interesting context for sociological understanding of economic processes of transformation with a long history of colonialism, economic nationalism, economic planning, and a dynamic transition from socialist-oriented mixed-economy to a full-fledged capitalism. Indian sociologists have been too preoccupied with the cultural perspective to the relative neglect of the structural focus on the 'economic'. Inexplicably, there is a paucity of Indian work on networks, markets, and firms from a sociological vantage point. A concerted focus on the market as an institution (and as an ideological construct) can very well be a productive point of departure for Indian sociology to compensate for its earlier neglect of studies of the economy.

Generally speaking, the 'market' is at the heart of new economic sociology. The understanding that social relations are fundamental to 'market processes' (Granovetter 1985: 500) has given rise to important empirical work in what is termed as new economic sociology (White 1981; Zelizer 1989; Baker and Faulkner 1993; Fligstein 2002; MacKenzie 2006). Whereas themes such as labour and industry have received fitful scholarly consideration from Indian sociologists, they did not find it worthwhile to study the economy and the market in terms of habits, customs, routines, and patterns, that is, to understand the broader questions of the production and maintenance of a market order. Such a project can look at the nature and the varying nuances of emerging forms of capitalism in developing countries and thereby contribute to an understanding of the comparative cultural foundations of Western capitalism (Beckert 2006). Likewise, Indian sociologists can fruitfully explore the promising area of culture, consumption, and markets in the context of a burgeoning middle class in India.

Curiously enough, the earlier sociological literature on themes such as factory, labour relations, trade unions, changing modes of production, and labour movement has also waned. There is lack of 'a healthy and robust tradition of sociological investigation in the industrial and corporate sectors notwithstanding the sub-discipline of industrial sociology'. Even today, 'there is no accessible text or research literature on the increasingly influential Indian managerial class' (Thakur 2017: 195). There is huge potential to sociologically capture the changes in the urban working especially in the post-liberalisation era. Indian sociology has much to gain by putting its focus on new forms of work and labour relations in a globally integrated economic order. Moreover, new substantive themes like 'gig economy' (with new modes of job flexibility and autonomy of the workers and firms) can serve as new arenas of sociological work. 'Social network' analysis is another worthy area of sociological enquiry into economic behaviour. Elsewhere, networks have been used as an analytical category to study topics as broad as mobility, competition, trust, migration, stress, occupational status, and the like. This line of enquiry can bring under sociological purview themes such as transnational migration, job search efforts, ethnic entrepreneurship, and local credit relations. Sociologists can equally focus on the role of values and emotions in economic transactions.

All this presupposes the need for a meaningful conversation across disciplinary boundaries. Institutions of management provide an ideal setting for such conversations to take place. These conversations are bound to enrich sociology's ability to expand beyond its usual institutional habitat of a university department. As Indian sociology enhances its scholarly engagement with an exciting range of economic phenomena, it acquires the ability to demonstrate its usefulness to management education and research. Management studies surely need sociologically grounded explanations of economic phenomena and processes in their myriad organisational and institutional manifestations.

One can see the tentative beginning of sociological engagement with economic processes and phenomena in the works of a new coven of scholars: Arjun Appadurai's (2015) work on the language and culture of business, Vasavi's (1996) work on managerial culture, Upadhya's (2004)

Conclusion 101

research on India's emerging transnational IT class; Panini's (1988) work on Indian managerial class and corporate culture, Mathur's (2019) work on consumer culture, Srivastava's (2014)work on metropolitan shopping malls, Kumar's (2016) work on Information Technology based market in rural India, Kapadia's (2016) (2017)scholarship on financial control and money and demonetisation, Kapadia and Jayadev's (2008) collaborative consideration of credit crisis, Chattaraj's (2015) writings on globalization, outsourcing, and informal vending, and Varman and Dholakia's (2020) work on consumption and the history of markets.

The field of management studies too is being pressurised into going for what could have been near impossible trade-offs a few years back. For instance, who would have imagined that Walmart would champion the cause of green energy and gay rights and lobby the U.S. government for more gun control laws? Clearly, Walmart is defying Milton Friedman's dictum that *business of business is business*. In a similar vein, many business leaders are giving Friedman's doctrine a decent burial by trying to think of customers, employees, other stakeholders, and the general aspects of human welfare and planetary health. These firms and businesses are not the embodiments of shareholders' value alone. They carry social responsibilities and not merely responsibilities to their shareholders. By bringing in added focus on employment, discrimination, pollution, ecological devastation, and the like, the new generation of managers and leaders are transgressing their earlier subservience to a firm owner's desire to make as much money as possible while conforming to the basic rules of society. The institution of the 'Business Roundtable' in the United States does articulate some of these new concerns regarding the essential purpose and value of management education. To the extent there is re-thinking and critical reflections on the essential mandate of management education with the promise of expanding its earlier rather myopic sense of remit, it has much to draw upon a discipline like sociology. In the ultimate analysis, a continued thickening of the engagement between sociology and management education will be to their mutual benefit.

Note

1. Economics has been an exception to this trend. Its sub-disciplines remain firmly lodged in its orbit as branches of economics without severing the umbilical cord with the parent discipline. Economics has managed to achieve this owing to its coherent disciplinary core, methodological monism, and parsimonious theoretical structure. In any case, there is greater consensus about what constitutes its core so that deviations get clubbed under heterodox economics.

References

Abbott, Andrew. 1988. *The System of Professions: An Essay on the Division of Expert Labour*. Chicago: University of Chicago Press.
Abbott, Andrew. 2001. *Chaos of Disciplines*. Chicago, IL: University of Chicago Press.
Abbott, Andrew. 2002. *Discipline and Department*. Chicago, IL: University of Chicago Press.
Abreu-Pederzini, Geraldo D., and Manuel F. Suárez-Barraza. 2020. "Just Let Us Be: Domination, the Postcolonial Condition and the Global Field of Business Schools". *Academy of Management Learning & Education* 19(1): 40–58.
Adler, Paul S., Glen Morgan Paul du Gay, and Michael Reed. eds. 2014. *The Oxford Handbook of Sociology, Social Theory and Organisation Studies*. Oxford: Oxford University Press.
Agarwal, R., and G. Hoetker. 2007. "A Faustian Bargain? The Growth of Management and Its Relationship with Related Disciplines". *The Academy of Management Journal* 50(6): 1304–1322.Alvesson, Mats, and Hugh Willmott. eds. 1992a. *Critical Management Studies*. London: Sage Publications.
Alvesson, Mats and Hugh Willmott (eds). 1992a. *Critical Management Studies*. London: Sage.
Alvesson, Mats, and Hugh Willmott. 1992b. "On the Idea of Emancipation in Management and Organizational Studies". *Academy of Management Review* 17(3): 432–464.
Alvesson, Mats, and Hugh Willmott. 1992c. "Critical Theory and Management Studies: An Introduction". In *Critical Management Studies* edited by Mats Alvesson and Hugh Willmott, 1–20. London: Sage.
Alvesson, Mats, and Hugh Willmott. eds. 2003. Studying Management Critically. London: Sage.
Alvesson, Mats, C. Hardy, and B. Harley. 2008. "Reflecting on Reflexivity: Reflexive Textual Practices in Organization and Management Theory". *Journal of Management Studies* 45: 480–501.
Alvesson, Mats, Tod Bridgman and Hugh Willmott. eds. 2009. Oxford Handbook of Critical Management Studies. New York: Oxford University Press.

References 103

Alvesson, Mats, and Hugh Willmott. eds. 2011. *Critical Management Studies 4 Vols*. London: Sage.

Alvesson, M., and H. Willmott. 2012. *Making Sense of Management*. 2nd ed. London: Sage.

Appadurai, Arjun. 2015. *Banking on Words: The Failure of Language in the Age of Derivative Finance*. Chicago: Chicago University Press.

Baker, W. E., and R. R. Faulkner. 1993. "The Social Organization of Conspiracy: Illegal Networks in the Heavy Electrical Equipment Industry". *American Sociological Review* 58(6): 837–860.

Balon, J., and J. Holmwood. 2019. "The Impossibility of Sociology as a Science: Arguments from within the Discipline". *Journal of Theory of Social Behaviour* 49: 334–347.

Bannister, Robert C. 1987. Sociology and Scientism: The American Quest for Objectivity, 1880–1940. Chapel Hill, NC: University of North Carolina Press.

Baritz, Loren. 1960. *Servants of Power: A History of the Use of Social Science in American Industry*. Middletown, CT: Wesleyan University Press.

Beckert, J. 2006. "Jens Beckert Answers Ten Questions about Economic Sociology". *Economic Sociology: The European Electronic Newsletter*, Max Planck Institute for the Study of Societies, Cologne 7(3): 34–39.

Bell, Daniel. 1956. *Work and Its Discontents: The Cult of Efficiency in America*. Boston: Beacon Press.

Berger, Peter L. 1992. "Sociology: A Disinvitation". *Society* 30: 12–18.

Bernstein, Basil. 2000. *Pedagogy, Symbolic Control and Identity*. London: Rowman & Littlefield.

Besio, Cristina, Paul du Gay, and Kathia Serrano Velarde. 2020. "Disappearing Organization: Reshaping the Sociology of Organization". *Critical Sociology* 68(4): 411–418.

Béteille, A. 2013. "Ourselves and Others". *Annual Review of Anthropology* 42: 1–16.

Beynon, Huw. 2011. "Engaging Labour: British Sociology 1945–2010". *Global Labour Journal* 2(1): 5–26.

Bhowmik, S. K. 2009. "India: Labour Sociology Searching for a Direction". *Work and Occupations* 36(2): 126–144.

Bliss, C. J., and N. Stern. 1982. *Palanpur: The Economy of an Indian Village*. Oxford: Oxford University Press.

Boltanski, L. 2011. *On Critique: A Sociology of Emancipation*. Oxford: Polity Press.

Bottomore, T. B. 1974. *Sociology as Social Criticism*. New York: Pantheon Books.

Bottomore, T. B. 2002. *The Frankfurt School and Its Critics*. London: Routledge.

Bourdieu, Pierre. 1996. *The State Nobility: Elite Schools in the Field of Power*. Stanford: Stanford University Press.

Breman, J. 1996. *Footloose Labour: Working in India's Informal Economy*. Cambridge: Cambridge University Press.

Brown, D., and M. J. Harrison. 1980. "The Demand for Relevance and the Role of Sociology in Business Studies Degrees". *Journal of Further and Higher Education* 4(3): 54–61.

Bruce, Kyle, and Chris Nyland. 2011. "Elton Mayo and the Deification of Human Relations". *Organisation Studies* 32(3): 383–405.

Burawoy, Michael. 2016. "Sociology as a Vocation". *Contemporary Sociology* 45(4): 379–393.

Butler, Nick, and Sverre Spoelstra. 2014. "The Regime of Excellence and the Erosion of Ethos in Critical Management Studies". *British Journal of Management* 25: 538–550.

Chakraborty, S. K. 1997. *Ethics in Management: Vedantic Perspective*. Delhi: Oxford University Press.

Chattaraj, Durba. 2015. "Globalization and Ambivalence: Rural Outsourcing in Southern Bengal". *International Labour and Working Class History* 87: 111–136.

Chatterjee, Debashis. 2012. *Timeless Leadership: 18 Leadership Sutras from the Bhagavad Gita*. London: John Wiley & Sons.

Chatterjee, N. 1982. "Industrial Relations in Management Education-A Case Study of the University of Delhi." Indian Journal of Industrial Relations 18(1): 43–58.

Chaturvedi, Anil, and Abha Chaturvedi. eds. 1995. *The Sociology of Formal Organisations*. New Delhi: Oxford University Press.

Clegg, S. R., M. Kornberger, C. Carter, and C. Rhodes. 2006. "For Management?". *Management Learning* 37: 7–27.

Collini, Stephan. 2012. *What Are Universities For?* London: Penguin Books.

Collini, Stephan. 2018. *Speaking of Universities*. London: Verso.

Connell, Raewyn. 2017. "In Praise of Sociology". *Cahiers de Recherche Sociologique* 54(3): 280–296.

Connell, Raewyn, Fran Collyer, Joao Maia, and Robert Morrell. 2017. "Toward a Global Sociology of Knowledge: Post-Colonial Reality and Intellectual Practices". *International Sociology* 32(1): 21–37.

Cooper, Geoff. 2012. "A Disciplinary Matter: Critical Sociology, Academic Governance and Interdisciplinarity". *Sociology* 47(1): 74–89.

Daston, Lorraine J., and Peter Galison. 2007. *Objectivity*. New York: Zone Books.

Davies, B. 2005. "The (Im)Possibility of Intellectual Work in Neoliberal Regimes". *Discourse* 26(1): 1–14.

Delbridge, Rick. 2014. "Promising Futures: Critical Management Studies, Post-Disciplinarity and the New Public Social Science". *Journal of Management Studies* 51(1): 95–117.

DeMartini, Joseph R. 1983. "Sociologists Working in Applied Settings." Sociological Perspectives 26(3): 341–351.

Deshpande, Satish. 2001. "Disciplinary Predicaments: Sociology and Anthropology in Postcolonial India". *Inter-Asia Cultural Studies* 2(2): 1–14.

Deshpande, Satish. 2018. "Anthropology in India". In *The International Encyclopedia of Anthropology* edited by H. Callan, 1–18. London: John Wiley & Sons Ltd.

Dube, S. C. 1958. *India's Changing Villages: Human Factors in Community*. London: Routledge & Kegan Paul.

References

Dumont, L., and D. Pocock. 1957. "For a Sociology of India". *Contributions to Indian Sociology* 1(1): 7–22.
Durkheim, E. 1982. *The Rules of Sociological Method*. London: Macmillan.
Eden, Dov. 2003. "From the Editors: Critical Management Studies and the Academy of Management Journal: Challenge and Counterchallenge". *The Academy of Management Journal* 46(4): 390–394. www.jstor.org/stable/30040634 Accessed on 16 September 2020.
Elger, Tony. 2009. "Teaching the Sociology of Work and Employment: Texts and Reflections". *Sociology* 43(5): 999–1006.
Epstein, T. S. 1973. *South India: Yesterday, Today and Tomorrow: Mysore Villages Revisited*. London: Macmillan.
Fligstein, N. 2002. *The Architecture of Markets: An Economic Sociology of Twenty-First-Century Capitalist Societies*. Princeton, NJ: Princeton University Press.
Ford, Jackie, Nancy Harding, and Mark Learmonth. 2010. "Who Is It That Would Make Business Schools More Critical? Critical Reflections on Critical Management Studies". *British Journal of Management* 21: 571–581.
Fournier, V., and C. Grey. 2000. "At the Critical Moment: Conditions and Prospects for Critical Management Studies". *Human Relations* 53: 7–32.
Freeman, Howard E. and Peter H. Rossi. 1984. "Furthering the Applied Side of Sociology." *American Sociological Review* 49(4): 571–580.
Gordon, R. A., and J. E. Howell. 1959. *Higher Education for Business*. New York: Columbia University Press.
Granovetter, M. 1985. "Economic Action and Social Structure: The Problem of Embeddedness". *American Journal of Sociology* 91(3): 481–510.
Grey, C. 2002. "What Are Business Schools Meant for? On Silence and Voice in Management Education". *Journal of Management Education* 26(5): 496–511.
Grey, Christopher. 2007. "Possibilities for Critical Management Education and Studies". *Scandinavian Journal of Management* 23: 463–471.
Grey, Christopher, and Hugh Willmott. 2005. *Critical Management Studies: A Reader*. New York: Oxford University Press.
Habermas, Jurgen. 1984. *The Theory of Communicative Action: Reason and the Rationalization of Society*. Boston: Beacon Press.
Hancock, Philip. 2008. "Critical Management Studies: An Introduction". *Critical Sociology* 34(1): 9–14.
Hauser, Philip M. 1961. "Aspects of Sociology for Business." *Sociological Enquiry* 31(2): 167–169.
Holmström, Mark. 1976. *South Indian Factory Workers: Their Life and Their World*. Cambridge: Cambridge University Press.
Holmwood, John. 2010. "Sociology's Misfortune: Disciplines, Interdisciplinarity and the Impact of Audit Culture". *British Journal of Sociology* 61(4): 639–658.
Holmwood, John. 2011. "Sociology after Fordism: Prospects and Problems". *European Journal of Social Theory* 14(4): 537–556.
Holmwood, John. 2014. "Beyond Capital? The Challenge for Sociology in Britain". *The British Journal of Sociology* 65(4): 607–618.
Hountondji, Paulin J. ed. 1997. *Endogenous Knowledge: Research Trails*. Dakar: CODESRIA.

Indian Institute of Management Calcutta. 1987. *Management Education and India: Collection of Convocation Addresses 1966–1987* (A Silver Jubilee Publication). Kolkata: IIMC.

Inglis, David. 2014. "What Is Worth Defending in Sociology Today? Presentism, Historical Vision and the Uses of Sociology". *Cultural Sociology* 8(1): 99–118.

Jammulamadaka, N. 2017. "A Postcolonial Critique of Indian's Management Education Scene". In *Management Education in India: Perspectives and Practices* edited by Manish Thakur and R. Rajesh Babu, 103–123. Singapore: Springer.

Jammulamadaka, N. 2019. "Author(ing) from Post-Colonial Context: Challenges and Jugaad Fixes". *Qualitative Research in Organizations and Management* 15(3): 388–401.

Joseph, Martin. 1991. *Sociology for Business: A Practical Approach*. London: Polity.

Joshi, P. C. 1969. "Agrarian Social Structure and Social Change". *Sankhyā: The Indian Journal of Statistics, Series B* 31(3/4): 479–490.

Kapadia, Anush. 2016. "Money and Demonetization: The Fetish of Fiat". *Economic and Political Weekly* 51(51). https://www.epw.in/journal/2016/51/perspectives/money-and-%E2%80%98demonetisation%E2%80%99.html Accessed on 22 October 2019.

Kapadia, Anush. 2017. "The Structure of State Borrowing: Towards a Political Theory of Control Mechanisms". *Cambridge Journal of Regions, Economy and Society* 10(1): 189–204.

Kapadia, Anush, and A. Jayadev. 2008. "The Credit Crisis: Where It Came from, What Happened, and How It Might End". *Economic and Political Weekly* 43(49): 33–41.

Khurana, Rakesh, and N. Nohria. 2008. 'It Is Time to Make Management a True Profession". *Harvard Business Review* 86(10): 70–77.

King, Anthony. 2007. "The Sociology of Sociology". *Philosophy of the Social Sciences* 37(4): 501–524.

Klikauer, Thomas. 2011. "Management and Emancipation: Two Opposing Ideas: *The Oxford Handbook of Critical Management Studies*". *International Journal of Social Economics* 38(6): 573–580.

Klikauer, Thomas. 2015a. "What Is Managerialism?". *Critical Sociology* 41(7–8): 1103–1119.

Klikauer, Thomas. 2015b. "Critical Management Research: Reflections from the Field". *Management Learning* 46(4): 501–504.

Klikauer, Thomas. 2015c. "Critical Management Studies and Critical Theory: A Review". *Capital and Class* 39(2): 197–220.

Klikauer, Thomas. 2018. "Critical Management as Critique of Management". *Critical Sociology* 44(4–5): 753–762.

Kohout, Jaroslav. 1968. "Sociology and Business Management". *Management International Review* 8(2–3): 89–91.

Kuhn, Thomas S. 1962. *The Structure of Scientific Revolutions*. Chicago: University of Chicago Press.

Kumar, R. 2016. *Rethinking Revolutions: Soyabean, Choupals, and the Changing Countryside in Central India*. New Delhi: Oxford University Press.

References

Latour, B. 2004. "Why Has Critique Run Out of Steam? From Matter of Fact to Matters of Concern". *Critical Inquiry* 30: 225–247.
Linstead, Steve. 1984. "Sociology in Business Studies Degrees". *Journal of Further and Higher Education* 8(2): 53–64.
Lipset, Seymour M. 1982. "The Academic Mind at the Top: The Political Behaviour and the Values of Faculty Elite". *Public Opinion Quarterly* 46: 143–168.
Livingston, J. S. 1971. "Myth of the Well-Educated Manager". *Harvard Business Review* 49(1): 79–89.
Llyod, Moya, and Andrew Thacker. 1997. *The Influence of Michel Foucault on Social Sciences and Humanities*. London: Palgrave-Macmillan.
Louch, A. R. 1963. "The Very Idea of a Social Science". *Inquiry: An Interdisciplinary Journal of Philosophy* 6(1–4): 273–286.
Machlup, Fritz. 1972. *Production and Distribution of Knowledge*. Princeton: Princeton University Press.
Machlup, Fritz. 1982. *Knowledge: Its Creation, Distribution and Economic Significance: The Branches of Learning* (Vol. 2). Princeton: Princeton University Press.
Machlup, Fritz. 1994. "Are the Social Sciences Really Inferior?" In *Readings in the Philosophy of Social Science* edited by Martin Michael and Lee C. McIntyre, 5–19. Cambridge, MA: The MIT Press.
MacKenzie, D. 2006. *An Engine, Not a Camera: How Financial Models Shape Markets*. Cambridge, MA: The MIT Press.
Mandjak, Tibor, and Zoltan Sazanto. 2010. "How Can Economic Sociology Help Business Relationship Management?". *Journal of Business and Industrial Marketing* 25(3): 202–208.
Mathur, Nita. 2019. *Consumer Culture, Modernity and Identity*. New Delhi: Sage.
Matthai, R. 1980. "The Organisation and the Institution: Management Education in India". *Economic and Political Weekly* 15(22): M69–M72.
Meyer, Marshall W. 1999. "Notes from a Border Discipline: Has the Border Become the Center". *Current Sociology* 28(5): 507–510.
Mignolo, Walter D. 2000. *Local Histories/Global Designs: Coloniality. Subaltern Knowledges*. Princeton: Princeton University Press.
Mignolo, Walter D. 2007. "Delinking: The Rhetoric of Modernity, the Logic of Coloniality and the Grammar of De-Coloniality". *Cultural Studies* 21(2–3): 449–514.
Mills, C. Wright. 1959. *The Sociological Imagination*. New York: Oxford University Press.
Morris, D. 1965. *The Emergence of an Industrial Labour Force in India: A Study of the Bombay Cotton Mills 1854–1947*. Berkeley: University of California Press.
Mukerjee, R. 1960. *The Philosophy of Social Science*. London: Macmillan and Co.
Mukerji, D. P. 1958. *Diversities: Essays in Economics, Sociology and Other Social Problems*. New Delhi: People's Publishing House.
Nisbet, Robert S. 1976. *Sociology as an Art Form*. London: Heinemann.

References

Panini, M. N. 1988. "Corporate Culture in India". *Economic and Political Weekly* 31(21): M86–M94.

Parker, Martin. 1995. "Critique in the Name of What? Postmodernism and Critical Approaches to Organization". *Organization Studies* 16: 553–564.

Parker, Martin. 2002. *Against Management: Organization in the Age of Managerialism*. Cambridge: Polity Press.

Parker, Martin. 2010. "The Sclerosis of Criticism: A Handbook of Critical Management Studies?" *Critical Policy Studies* 4(3): 297–302.

Parker, Martin. 2013. "'What Is to Be Done?' CMS as a Political Party". *Dialogues in Critical Management Studies* 2: 165–181.

Parker, Martin. 2014. "Between Sociology and the Business School: Critical Studies of Work, Employment and Organization in the UK". *The Sociological Review* 63(1): 162–180.

Parry, J. P. 1999. "Lords of Labour: Working and Shirking in Bhilai". *Contributions to Indian Sociology* 33(1–2): 107–140.

Parsons, Talcott. 1937. *The Structure of Social Action: A Study in Social Theory with Special Reference to a Group of Recent European Writers*. Glencoe, IL: The Free Press.

Parush, T. 2008. "From "Management Ideology" to "Management Fashion": A Comparative Analysis of Two Key Concepts in the Sociology of Management Knowledge". *International Studies of Management and Organization* 38: 48–70.

Patel, S. 1998. "The Nostalgia for the Village: M. N. Srinivas and the Making of Indian Social Anthropology". *South Asia: Journal of South Asian Studies* 21(1): 49–61.

Pierson, F. C. 1959. *The Education of American Businessmen*. New York: McGraw-Hill.

Planning Commission. 1957. *Second Five Year Plan: Education and Social Services*. Delhi: Planning Commission, Government of India.

Ramnath, Aparajith. 2017. *The Birth of an Indian Profession: Engineers, Industry and the State, 1900–1947*. Delhi: Oxford University Press.

Reed, Mike. 1985. "Reflections on 'Realist Turn' in Organization and Management Studies". *Journal of Management Studies* 42(8): 1621–1644.

Robbins, George W. 1959. *Recommendations for an All-Indian Institute of Management*. New Delhi: The Ford Foundation.

Rowlinson, M., and J. Hassard. 2000. "Marxist Political Economy, Revolutionary Politics, and Labor Process Theory". *International Studies of Management and Organization* 30(4): 85–111.

Saberwal, S. 1982. "Uncertain Transplants: Anthropology and Sociology in India". *Ethnos* 47(1–2): 36–49.

Saha, B. 2005. "Cross-Cultural Studies in Management". *Economic and Political Weekly* 40(29): 3138–3139.

Santos, Boaventura de Souza. 2014. *Epistemologies of the South: Justice Against Epistemicide*. Boulder, CO: Paradigm Publishers.

Savage, Mike. 2010. "Unpicking Sociology's Misfortunes". *British Journal of Sociology* 61(4): 659–665.

Scott, J. 2005. "Sociology and Its Others: Reflections on Disciplinary Specialisation and Fragmentation". *Sociological Research Online* 10(1). https://www.sourcesonline.org.uk/10/1/scott.html Accessed on 28 June 2019.

Scott, Alan. 2020. "Prodigal Offspring: Organizational Sociology and Organisation Studies". *Sociology* 68(4): 443–458.

Sharma, B. R. 1974. *The Indian Industrial Worker: Issues in Perspective*. Delhi: Vikas Publications.

Sheth, N. R. 1977. "Sociological Studies of Indian Industrial Workers". *Sociological Bulletin* 26(1): 76–90.

Sheth, N. R. 1991. "What Is Wrong with Management Education". *Economic and Political Weekly* 26(48): M123–M128.

Sheth, N. R. 1996. "We, the Trade Unions". *Indian Journal of Industrial Relations* 36(4): 1–20.

Smith, J. H. 1960. "Sociology and Management Studies". *British Journal of Sociology* 11(2): 103–111.

Smith, J. H. 1998. "The Enduring Legacy of Elton Mayo." *Human Relations* 51: 221–249.

Sodhi, J. S., and Daniel H. Plowman. 2002. "The Study of Industrial Relations: A Changing Field". *Indian Journal of Industrial Relations* 37(4): 459–485.

Spicer, A., M. Alvesson, and D. Kärreman. 2009. "Critical Performativity: The Unfinished Business of Critical Management Studies". *Human Relations* 62: 537–560.

Srinivas, M. N. 1994. "Sociology in India and Its Future". *Sociological Bulletin* 43(1): 9–19.

Srinivas, M. N., and M. N. Panini. 1973. "The Development of Sociology and Social Anthropology in India". *Sociological Bulletin* 22(2): 179–215.

Srivastava, Sanjay. 2014. *Entangled Urbanism: Slum, Gated Community and Shopping Mall in Delhi and Gurgaon*. Oxford: Oxford University Press.

Starkey, K., and N. Tiratsoo. 2007. *The Business School and the Bottom Line*. Cambridge: Cambridge University Press.

Surendran, Aardra. 2018. "Notes towards a Renewal of Industrial Sociology in India". In *Doing Theory: Locations, Hierarchies and Disjunctions* edited by Maitrayee Chaudhuri and Manish Thakur, 127–48. Hyderabad: Orient Blackswan.

Tatli, Ahu. 2012. "On the Power and Poverty of Critical (Self) Reflection in Critical Management Studies: A Comment on Ford, Harding and Learmonth". *British Journal of Management* 23: 22–30.

Taylor, F.W. 1911. *The Principles of Scientific Management*. New York: Harper and Brothers.Thakur, Manish K. 2006. "Social Scientists or Development Professionals? Research-Policy Interface in a Rural Development Institute". *Review of Development and Change* 11(2): 179–200.

Thakur, Manish. 2010. "Of Mainstream and Margins: Sociology in Indian Institutes of Management (IIMs)". In *Sociology in India: Intellectual and Institutional Practises* edited by Maitrayee Chaudhuri, 157–180. Jaipur: Rawat Publishers.

Thakur, Manish. 2014a. *Indian Village: A Conceptual History*. Jaipur: Rawat Publications.

Thakur, Manish. 2014b. *The Quest for Indian Sociology: Radhakamal Mukerjee and Our Times*. Shimla: Indian Institute of Advanced Study.

Thakur, Manish. 2017. "(Invisible) Disciplines: Sociology and Management". In *Management Education in India: Perspectives and Practices* edited by Manish Thakur and R. Rajesh Babu, 183–199. Singapore: Springer.

Thapan, M. 1988. "Contributions and the Sociology of India". *Contributions to Indian Sociology* 22(2): 259–272.

Therbon, Goran. 2000. "At the Birth of Second Century Sociology: Times of Reflexivity, Spaces of Identity and Nodes of Knowledge". *British Journal of Sociology* 51(1): 37–57.

Thomas, Howard, Peter Lorange, and Jagdish Sheth. 2013. *The Business School in the Twenty-First Century: Emergent Challenges and New Business Models*. Cambridge: Cambridge University Press.

Thompson, P. 2004. "Brand, Boundaries and Bandwagons: A Critical Reflection on Critical Management Studies". In *Critical Management Studies: A Reader* edited by Christopher Grey and H. Willmott, 364–381. Oxford: Oxford University Press.

Thompson, Paul. 2011. "The Trouble with HRM". *Human Resource Management Journal* 21(4): 355–367.

Thrift, Nigel. 2005. *Knowing Capitalism*. London: Sage.

Upadhya, C. 2004. "A New Transnational Capitalist Class? Capital Flows, Business Networks and Entrepreneurs in the Indian Software Industry". *Economic and Political Weekly* 39(48): 5141–5151.

Urry, John. 1995. *Consuming Places*. London: Routledge.

Vaara, Eero. 2011. "On the Importance of Broader Critique: Discursive Knowledge Production in Management Education". *British Journal of Management* 22: 564–566.

Varman, Rohit, and Biswatosh Saha. 2009. "Disciplining the Discipline: Understanding Postcolonial Epistemic Ideology in Marketing". *Journal of Marketing Management* 25(7–8): 811–824.

Varman, Rohit, Biswatosh Saha, and Per Skålén. 2011. "Market Subjectivity and Neoliberal Governmentality in Higher Education". *Journal of Marketing Management* 27(11–12): 1163–1185.

Varman, Rohit, and Devi Vijay. 2018. "Dispossessing Vulnerable Consumers: Derealization, Desubjectification and Violence". *Marketing Theory* 18(3): 307–326.

Varman, Rohit, and Nikhilesh Dholakia. 2020. "Special Issue on History of Indian Marketing". *Journal of Historical Research in Marketing* 10(3).

Varman, Rohit, Paromita Goswami, and Devi Vijay. 2018. "The Precarity of Respectable Consumption: Normalizing Sexual Violence Against Women". *Journal of Marketing Management* 34(5): 1–33.

Vasavi, A. R. 1996. "Co-Opting Culture: Managerialism in an Age of Consumer Capitalism". *Economic and Political Weekly* 31(21). https://www.epw.in/journal/1996/21/review-industry-and-management-uncategorised/co-opting-culture-managerialism-age Accessed on 14 September 2019.

Venkateswaran, R. T., and A. K. Ojha. 2017. "Strategic Management Research on Emerging Economies: Cultural Imperialism in Universalizing Research Paradigms". *Critical Perspectives on International Business* 13(3): 204–225.

Vijay, Devi. 2019. "Special Issue on Changing Nature of Work and Organisations in India". *Decision* 46(2): 93–97.

Vijay, Devi, and Rohit Varman. 2017. *Undoing Boundaries: Alternative Organisations in India*. Cambridge: Cambridge University Press.

Vikas, Ram M., Rohit Varman, and Russell W. Belk. 2015. "Status, Caste, and Markets in a Changing Indian Village". *Journal of Consumer Research* 42(3): 472–498.

White, H. C. 1981. "Where Do Markets Come From?". *American Journal of Sociology* 87(3): 517–547.

Winch, Peter. 1958. *The Idea of Social Science and Its Relation to Philosophy*. London: Routledge.

Zald, Mayer N. 2002. "Spinning Disciplines: Critical Management Studies in the Context of the Transformation of the Management Education". *Organization* 9(3): 365–385.

Zelizer, V. A. 1989. "The Social Meaning of Money: 'Special Monies'". *American Journal of Sociology* 95(2): 342–377.

Index

AACSB 30
Abbott, Andrew 6, 11, 20–21, 95, 102
academic disciplines 4–7, 9–10, 15, 29–30, 32, 37, 39, 43, 48–49, 53, 68, 77, 79, 94, 97
AICTE 44
AIMA 44
AMBA 34

Berger, Peter 18, 83, 103
Bologna Accord 34
Boltanski, L. 8, 103
Bourdieu, Pierre 5, 97, 103

Carnegie Foundation 31–32
Collini, Stephan 6–7, 53, 104
Cow Sociology 72
critical discipline 61, 66, 71, 97
critters 83

decolonisation of Indian mind 44
Durkheim, Emile 15, 19, 22, 104

EQUIS 34
extroversion 96

Ford Foundation 31–32, 36, 43
fractal discipline 6, 11
Frankfurt School 81
Franks Report 31

Global South 96
Grey, Christopher 1, 35–36, 38, 73–75, 77–78, 86, 88, 90, 92, 105

Habermas, Jurgen 21, 75, 81, 97, 105
Hawthorne experiments 25, 40, 69
heterodox sociology 17
Hountondji, Paulin 96, 105

ICSSR 51
IIM Ahmedabad 32, 46, 55
IIM Bangalore 55
IIM Calcutta 32, 43, 46
IIMs (Indian Institutes of Management) 9, 32, 45–48, 56
IITs 41–43, 45
Indian sociology 41, 51, 57–58, 61–66, 99–100
indigenisation 44
INSEAD 34

Kuhn, Thomas S. 6, 69, 106

labour process theory (Henry Braverman) 70, 77
Latour, B. 22, 106
London Business School 34–35

Machlup, Fritz 5, 6, 14, 53, 107
Mayo, Elton 25, 39–40, 69
Mignolo, Walter D. 83, 96, 107
Mode 2 7–8, 16, 97

NIRF (National Institutional Ranking Framework) 7
Nisbet, Robert S. 58, 83, 107

OBCs (Other Backward Classes) 42
origins of management education 29–31

Parker, Martin 70–72, 75, 80, 82–83, 86, 90, 93, 107–108
Patel, S. 63, 108
principles of scientific management 27, 37
PSUs 44

REF (Research Excellence Framework) 7

Simon, Herbert 30–31
Sloan School of Management 32, 46

social facts 15
southern theory 85
Srinivas, M.N. 18, 61–62, 108–109
sub-prime crisis 27

Taylor, F.W. 27, 37, 109
Therborn, Goran 17–18, 110

UGC 51

Wharton Business School 29
Winch, Peter 22, 111
Work, Employment and Society 78

Zald, Mayer N. 4–6, 9–10, 12, 80, 85, 89, 111